What a treasure of a book! The teaching,
chotherapy are enhanced when we openly
and continuously process "taboo" topics th
authors provide history and sources of res

identity, anger, oppression, and sexual feelings regarding clients. Most importantly, and of significant value, the book provides strategies that inspire us to have the courage, confidence, and determination to address the relevant issues in the various contexts in which we work. After reading this outstanding, compelling, must-read contribution, you will agree that creating a culture of speaking up benefits us all!

—**Melba J. T. Vasquez, PhD, ABPP,** Independent Practice; Former President, American Psychological Association

Here, at last, is the book we never really knew we needed, but needed so desperately. "Silence and silencing have shaped the psychotherapy profession." Truer words were never (un)spoken.

—**Eric Y. Drogin, JD, PhD, ABPP,** Harvard Medical School, Boston, MA, United States; Former Chair, APA Committee on Professional Practice and Standards

Speaking the Unspoken is essential reading for anyone who practices, teaches, supervises, and studies psychotherapy. It will help you to recognize and overcome barriers to thinking clearly, speaking openly, and listening respectfully about unspoken topics in our profession. The engaging vignettes, thought-provoking exercises, suggested strategies, and informational pearls of wisdom will strengthen your courage, humility, readiness, and skills to engage in authentic discussions.

—**Joan Cook, PhD,** Professor of Psychology, Yale University, New Haven, CT, United States

Kenneth S. Pope, the foremost psychological ethicist of our time (someone who walks the talk), and a diverse and distinguished cadre of coauthors provide a necessary exploration of censored and challenging topics in psychotherapy. They show how correct Sigmund Freud was in positing that suppressed material will "come forth later in uglier ways."

—**Etzel Cardeña, PhD,** Thorsen Professor in Psychology, Lund University, Lund, Sweden; Coeditor, *Varieties of Anomalous Experience;* founding editor, *Journal of Anomalous Experience and Cognition*

Speaking the Unspoken: Breaking the Silence, Myths and Taboos That Hurt Therapists and Patients is a must-read for EVERY therapist. The authors raise awareness and brilliantly illustrate how to address critical, contemporary, and challenging issues in therapy and supervision, including oppression and racism. I highly recommend this book.

—**Lillian Comas-Díaz, PhD,** Recipient of the American Psychological Association Gold Medal Award for Life Achievement in the Practice of Psychology; Past President, Psychologists in Independent Practice, APA Division 42; Author of *Multicultural Care: A Clinician's Guide to Cultural Competence*

Have you ever avoided talking about something important? Have you ever wished for the courage to speak up? In clear and accessible prose, *Speaking the Unspoken* explains what underlies the fear and the other obstacles that keep us silent. With remarkable clarity, the book models the courage to discuss complex topics and provides practical advice for how and when to discuss previously unspoken matters. Every psychotherapist should read this intelligent and transformative book.

—**Jennifer Joy Freyd, PhD,** Founder and President, Center for Institutional Courage; Professor Emerit, Psychology, University of Oregon, Eugene, OR; Adjunct Professor, Psychiatry & Behavioral Sciences, Stanford University, Stanford, CA, United States; Editor, *Journal of Trauma & Dissociation*

Brave and compelling, Pope and colleagues' volume paves the way for change and enlightenment of mindsets in clinical training, supervision, and practice. This courageous book outlines what is NOT DISCUSSED in clinical practice, supervision, and consultation; the impacts of these omitted topics; and guideposts to identify, reflect on, and address them. The authors address emotionally, politically, and personally charged topics that are avoided. It is a "must-read" for educators, supervisors, and clinicians-in-training.

—**Carol Falender, PhD**, Adjunct Professor, Graduate School of Education and Psychology, Pepperdine University, Los Angeles, CA; Clinical Professor, Psychology Department, University of California, Los Angeles, Los Angeles, CA, United States; Coauthor, Coeditor of six books on Competency-Based Clinical Supervision, one on Competency-Based Consultation

"Several topics have been historically avoided in psychotherapy." The opening line of this book sheds light on a central truth—we tend to avoid certain topics because we have been told it is "uncultured" to address them in "polite society." Although we may wish it to be so, averting our gaze does not remove these issues and problems from reality—not in society and not in our practices. The authors, experts in ethics, multiculturalism, practice, and training, do an excellent job of guiding us through our own necessary edification. They invite us not to collude with the silence and the avoidance created when we hide behind the veil of "politeness" and the guise of clinical neutrality. The book aims to enhance our skills and tolerance to feeling distressed and uncomfortable when we do "Break the Silence." In learning how to do the necessary yet uncomfortable, we benefit our profession and the people we serve.

—**Cynthia de las Fuentes, PhD**, Independent Practice

SPEAKING the UNSPOKEN

SPEAKING the UNSPOKEN

Breaking the Silence, Myths, and Taboos That Hurt Therapists and Patients

Kenneth S. Pope

Nayeli Y. Chavez-Dueñas

Hector Y. Adames

Janet L. Sonne

Beverly A. Greene

 AMERICAN PSYCHOLOGICAL ASSOCIATION

Published by
American Psychological Association
750 First Street, NE
Washington, DC 20002
https://www.apa.org

Order Department
https://www.apa.org/pubs/books
order@apa.org

Typeset in Charter and Interstate by Circle Graphics, Inc., Reisterstown, MD

Printer: Gasch Printing, Odenton, MD
Cover Designer: Anthony Paular Design, Newbury Park, CA

Library of Congress Cataloging-in-Publication Data

Names: Pope, Kenneth S., author. | Chavez-Dueñas, Nayeli Y., author. |
  Adames, Hector Y., author. | Sonne, Janet L., author. | Greene, Beverly, author.
Title: Speaking the unspoken : breaking the silence, myths, and taboos that
  hurt therapists and patients / by Kenneth S. Pope, Nayeli Y. Chavez-Dueñas,
  Hector Y. Adames, Janet L. Sonne, and Beverly A. Greene.
Description: Washington, DC : American Psychological Association, [2023] |
  Includes bibliographical references and index.
Identifiers: LCCN 2022051587 (print) | LCCN 2022051588 (ebook) |
  ISBN 9781433841590 (paperback) | ISBN 9781433841606 (ebook)
Subjects: LCSH: Psychotherapists. | Psychotherapist and patient. |
  Psychotherapy--Moral and ethical aspects. | Freedom of expression. |
  BISAC: PSYCHOLOGY / Psychotherapy / Counseling | PSYCHOLOGY /
  Clinical Psychology
Classification: LCC RC480.8 .P664 2023 (print) | LCC RC480.8 (ebook) |
  DDC 616.89/14--dc23/eng/20230106
LC record available at https://lccn.loc.gov/2022051587
LC ebook record available at https://lccn.loc.gov/2022051588

https://doi.org/10.1037/0000350-000

Printed in the United States of America

10 9 8 7 6 5 4 3 2 1

For all those who spoke up when the costs were high, when others couldn't or didn't, and when it counted. For my dear friends who share the good times, help me through the bad times, and make sure we have plenty of music, singing, and laughs along the way. For my sister Katherine, who has always been there with unfailing love, support, and encouragement. And for Karen, the magical love of my life, who, every day since we met, makes me feel I am the luckiest person on earth.
—KENNETH S. POPE

Para Itzael Ali, mi niño adorado. Te amo sin medida y prometo dedicar mi vida para construir el mundo en que merezcas vivir, un mundo sin odio y sin racismo donde puedas se quién eres y ser amado y por serlo. Este libro, mi trabajo y mi vida entera te los dedico a ti. Uémbekua! Para mi madre hasta el cielo, y para mi familia y mi comunidad inmigrante; por ustedes soy quien soy.
[For Itzael Ali, my beloved boy. I love you beyond measure, and I promise to dedicate my life to building the world you deserve to live in, a world without hate and without racism where you can be who you are and be loved for being so. I dedicate this book, my work, and my entire life to you. Uémbekua! For my mother up in heaven and for my family and my immigrant community; because of you, I am who I am.]
—NAYELI Y. CHAVEZ-DUEÑAS

To Mami, Papi, and Mama Bache. Thank you for teaching me the importance of questioning, speaking up, and dancing in a changing world. We exist. We are valuable. We are people of determination. Our cries and dreams are always about our people's liberation. Gracias por dármelo todo. [Thank you for giving me everything.]
—HECTOR Y. ADAMES

And the secret garden bloomed and bloomed, and every morning revealed new miracles.

—Frances Hodgson Burnett, *The Secret Garden*, Published by J. B. Lippincott in 1949 (p. 250)

I dedicate my part in the creation of this book to all who have taught me how to honor and nurture potential, learning, and growth: my parents; husband; children; grandchildren; siblings; college roommates; friends; instructors and supervisors; students; and, particularly on this project, my coauthors. Each has contributed in their unique ways to my garden full of green and blooms and miracles. I leave my wish for Paige, Jane, Claire, Alaina, Gus, and Meg that you may each discover your own secret garden.

—JANET L. SONNE

To my beloved parents, other mothers, and wise elders. Born and raised in the depths of American racial apartheid, they were role models for their intelligence and compassion and for managing indignities with dignity, humor, and grace. They did not hesitate to love us deeply and to speak truths in the face of distortions about who we were, who we came from, and what we could be. For their empowering lesson that everything we do or fail to do matters because the future has not been written and the last word has not been spoken. Their mantra for us always urged, "You have to live your life and live it fully, and in the face of inevitable obstacles, Just keep moving forward!"

—BEVERLY A. GREENE

Contents

Acknowledgments

The book you're holding in your hands or seeing on your screens would never have existed had the remarkable Susan Reynolds at the American Psychological Association (APA) not reached out to us with the idea that we write a book on this topic. Our editorial dream team at APA, Kristen Knight, Rohita Atluri, and Laurel Vincenty, provided everything we needed and offered encouragement, guidance, expertise, tolerance, and support. If you find this book useful. . . . But, wait! We're confident we can do away with that conditional "if" and restart this sentence: *When* you find this book useful, please know that Susan, Kristen, Rohita, and Laurel deserve a lot of the credit.

We also want to acknowledge and thank the many special individuals and communities—professors, supervisors, mentors, colleagues, patients, students, friends, family, and professional and social groups and organizations—that nurtured, challenged, and sustained us, helping each of us reach the point when we were able to write this particular book. You, too, deserve a large share of the credit.

Thank you to the anonymous reviewers who generously took the time to read our evolving manuscript and lend their wisdom, judgment, and expertise.

Our talented students, Paola Mendoza and Madeleine Ally, provided excellent help with the tiresome and unexciting challenge of making sure the references were complete and accurate. We deeply appreciate their conscientious, meticulous, and good-humored approach to a task that inevitably includes frustrations known to drive meditation masters to rip off their tranquility beads and stomp their serenity bowls into a million pieces.

SPEAKING the
UNSPOKEN

INTRODUCTION

Unspoken Topics in Psychotherapy and How This Book Can Help Break the Silence

The practice of psychotherapy has an unfortunate history of maintaining silence around certain topics. Difficulty thinking clearly and speaking openly, honestly, and directly about these topics continues to plague the practice of psychotherapy. We—those of us who practice, teach, supervise, and study psychotherapy—may not often think about the "unspoken" topics. We may swerve around the silence as if it were a deadly threat. We may lapse into absurdly abstract language to keep these topics at a safe distance. We may fill the air with distractions and distortions. We may shroud the unspoken with familiar myths. We may simply keep our mouths shut, not saying what we know to be important, relevant, and true.

This book discusses how these various forms of silence undermine, stunt, and derail the teaching, practice, and profession of psychotherapy. It also considers how those of us who love the profession and have dedicated our lives to it can recognize, understand, and overcome the barriers to speaking about them frankly and realistically. We share information, approaches, and strategies for how to think about, reflect on, and engage with these unspoken topics regardless of our professional context and setting (e.g., university, professional

https://doi.org/10.1037/0000350-001
Speaking the Unspoken: Breaking the Silence, Myths, and Taboos That Hurt Therapists and Patients, by K. S. Pope, N. Y. Chavez-Dueñas, H. Y. Adames, J. L. Sonne, and B. A. Greene

school, and continuing education courses; our individual practices of psycho-therapy, counseling, supervision, and consultation; our research; our forensic work as expert or fact witnesses).

We specifically focus on topics that often fall prey to various forms of silence, including

- physical difference and disability,
- sexual and affectional (romantic) orientation,
- sexual reactions to clients,
- therapist feelings of anger,
- oppression,
- White supremacy culture,
- religion,
- money and fees, and
- death and dying.

The book comprises 18 chapters organized into five sections.[1] Part I intro-duces the problem of the unspoken in psychotherapy. Our ability to think clearly and speak openly, honestly, and directly depends on acknowledging and addressing the current social, cultural, and political contexts in which we find ourselves as individuals and professionals. Chapter 1 focuses on these external events and forces, including cancel culture, hyperpolarization, legisla-tion to ban books and specific topics, and academics who report on anonymous surveys that they are afraid to address certain subjects in their teaching. These circumstances lead many of us to resort to self-censorship in one area or another. They choke off our impulse to speak up and speak out. They sap our ability to connect with our patients, students, and colleagues. We have difficulty expressing ourselves freely and listening respectfully to those who disagree about controversial issues.

Understanding how challenging topics came to be silenced also depends, to some extent, on viewing them in their historical context. However tempting it may be to gloss over historical details, an accurate view of how the profession has mishandled these topics can help us in our attempts to avoid repeating the mistakes of the past. As Santayana (1905) famously wrote, "Those who cannot remember the past are condemned to repeat it" (p. 284). Thus, Chapter 2 discusses historical examples of how silence and myths were harmful to clients

---

[1]This book is different from (i.e., not a new edition of) but in the tradition of two prior books: *Sexual Feelings in Psychotherapy: Explorations for Therapists and Therapists-in-Training* (Pope et al., 1993) and *What Therapists Don't Talk About and Why: Understanding Taboos That Hurt Us and Our Clients* (Pope et al., 2006).

and the process of psychotherapy. Chapter 3 examines cognitive cues for keeping quiet and how they fit in with systems of silencing and other barriers to speaking up. In Chapter 4, we explore in more detail the profession's bleak history of denial, resistance, and distortions in the realm of therapists' sexual feelings and behavior with clients. This history not only helps us understand issues involving therapists' sexual feelings and behavior and how the profession responds to these issues but also prompts questions about the extent to which the silence and myths may continue in different forms and settings.

Although, at least according to Santayana (1905), failure to remember this history guarantees that we will repeat it, learning this history and keeping it in mind can *help*, but it does not guarantee that we will not fall into the same traps. A character in a Kurt Vonnegut (1987) novel says that she's got news for Santayana: that we can be doomed to repeat the past event if we remember it because that's what it means to be human. Faulkner (1950/2011) had a different caution regarding our belief that we can easily or definitively escape the past and its mistakes: "The past is never dead. It's not even past" (p. 73).

Part II is designed to help prepare therapists to break the silence. Chapter 5 provides a self-assessment as a prelude to Chapter 6, which walks the reader through the process of creating practical conditions for learning and strengthening our skills at speaking up. That chapter also introduces the exercises provided in Part III along with suggestions about how to work on those exercises.

In Part III, Chapters 7 through 15 offer exercises for exploring and learning. Through these exercises, therapists can practice confronting and speaking openly, honestly, and directly about the difficult topics listed earlier.

Part IV takes us beyond the realm of psychotherapy. It addresses speaking up in supervision and consultation (Chapter 16) and throughout the profession and the community (Chapter 17).

Part V, the final section, discusses strategies for moving forward when things do not go as planned as we work to speak up.

Throughout the text, readers will find questions, vignettes, and scenarios designed to encourage deep reflection about these topics as they relate to psychotherapy. All vignettes and scenarios have been vetted to ensure confidentiality.

The purpose of this book is to promote *understanding* of (a) unspoken and silenced topics; (b) the profession's history around these areas; and (c) the relevant research regarding the cognitive and other internal factors that play a role in self-silencing as well as the social, organizational, and other external silencing factors.

In addition, we seek to promote *action* by presenting specific strategies for summoning and practicing the courage, confidence, and determination to speak more openly, honestly, and directly in the therapy office, the classroom, and the courtroom, and in the community. Each of us can do our part to break the silence and expose the myths and distortions that have plagued our profession. We can bring about more openness, curiosity, and frank, respectful discussion in our education and our clinical, forensic, and community work.

Let's begin the conversation! Ready to join us?

PART **I** THE PROBLEM OF
THE UNSPOKEN

1

A CHILLING CONTEXT FOR PSYCHOTHERAPY

Cancel Culture, Hyperpolarization, Books and Topics Banned by the State, Frightened Academics, and Self-Censorship

Most psychotherapy courses and textbooks focus on the therapist, the patient, and what happens during the therapy session. It is as if therapy occurs in a vacuum. We may spend little time studying and discussing the political and other environmental factors that create the context in which therapist and patient live their lives and therapy takes place. But these contexts can cause profound effects on therapists, patients, and the process of therapy. Consider the following four vignettes and set of questions, reflecting on the social contexts that can make it hard to approach taboo topics like those explored in Part III of this book.

VIGNETTE 1

Imagine you are a politically conservative student in a psychotherapy training program in which the faculty and other students are enthusiastically liberal. Consider these questions:

- How, if at all, do you believe that might affect what you choose to say or remain silent about?

https://doi.org/10.1037/0000350-002
Speaking the Unspoken: Breaking the Silence, Myths, and Taboos That Hurt Therapists and Patients, by K. S. Pope, N. Y. Chavez-Dueñas, H. Y. Adames, J. L. Sonne, and B. A. Greene

- In what way, if at all, would politics affect how other students and faculty view and respond to what you said?

- In what way, if at all, would that political difference affect what you learned about psychotherapy and how you learned it?

- Do you believe there are any significant differences in assumptions about patients, their problems, and what kinds of interventions are likely to be helpful and appropriate between a hypothetical graduate program in which the faculty and students are overwhelmingly conservative and one in which faculty and students are overwhelmingly liberal?
  - Which program would you rather attend or teach at? Why?
  - Which program do you think would do a better job of training students to serve the needs of their clients? Why?

VIGNETTE 2

A new client talks about wanting to kill themselves. As part of your assessment, you ask whether they have ready access to the means, including whether they have guns in their house, which is in Florida. Consider these questions:

- Would the political views of therapist and patient potentially impact what happens next?

- The client responds, "You have no right to ask me that," an idea they may have gotten from a Florida law, which the National Rifle Association lobbied for and was signed into effect in 2011. That law put limits on doctors asking about patients' guns and ammunition, with penalties including loss of license. Six years later, an appellate court overturned the law as unconstitutional interference with the freedom of speech (Rozel et al., 2021; Simonetti et al., 2021; Wintemute et al., 2016). Are you aware of any limits or restraints on what a psychotherapist can ask or say to a patient in your particular state?

- What do you think you would say next to the client?

VIGNETTE 3

You've been invited to deliver a lecture to the faculty and students of a psychotherapy training program that you desperately hope will hire you. Consider these questions:

- As you plan this audition, are there any unpopular, controversial, or risky ideas you would avoid because they might undermine your chances of being hired?

- Suppose the internal politics of the training program treat certain ideas as off limits for discussion. How, if at all, do you believe that affects the educational process and the views and competence of the therapists who graduate from that program?

- What ideas, views, or questions do you believe are off limits in training programs, professional conferences, or journals?
  - How, if at all, do you think this affects the profession, education, and scholarship?
  - How, if at all, would it influence how we think about and conduct psychotherapy?

VIGNETTE 4

A client who never wanted to have children is barely scraping by financially. She cannot afford to support a child. She tells you, however, that her birth control failed, and she is now pregnant. The client wants to spend the session discussing her situation, options, and what she wants to do. Consider these questions:

- What difference, if any, does it make whether you practice in a *red state* (where voters mainly vote for the Republican Party) or *blue state* (where voters mainly vote for the Democratic Party)?

- Would there be any special considerations about what you put into the client's chart about this session?

- As you think about the politics in your state and the kinds of laws it has created, how, if at all, do you think politics might affect the client, therapist, and the psychotherapy process in this vignette, either directly or indirectly?

OUR ROLE AND RESPONSIBILITY IN SPEAKING ABOUT TABOO SUBJECTS

Cultural, political, and similar contexts can greatly shape our training and practice as psychotherapists. They can make it difficult, dangerous, unwise, or costly to discuss or even acknowledge some topics despite how central these topics may be to treatment.

Suppose we are to speak openly, honestly, and directly about topics that affect our training and work as psychotherapists. In that case, we'll need to set aside the common tendency to replace genuine discussion with each person rotely repeating—sometimes louder and louder—their own hardened positions and well-worn talking points. This predictable pattern includes little or no willingness to engage, encourage, appreciate, or learn. Instead, "listening" becomes impatiently waiting for the other person to finish while scanning whatever they say for ammunition that can be turned against them or trying to think of ways to shut down and shut up those who disagree.

We'll need to be alert to other popular means of preventing open, honest, and candid discussions. Some examples include quickly stopping conversation by distracting or interrupting someone trying to introduce a taboo topic, halting the discussion, or simply withdrawing in silence. If we don't learn and practice exploring this array of taboo topics during our training, we'll find ourselves unprepared to raise and discuss them effectively in our work with our patients.

This chapter highlights current cultural trends that work against the context of good therapy—a context that seeks to open the inquiry between therapist and client and allow exploration of any topic regardless of whether their perspectives are shared or different. Our work as therapists is *not to* change the patient's opinion or persuade them that our viewpoint is correct. Instead, our job is to understand the patient's perspective so that it can be considered in the development of the treatment plan. Becoming and remaining aware of the strategies of avoidance, denial, and silencing that these cultural trends foster and how these strategies deter, distort, and dissolve discussions can help us counter and overcome their influence.

CANCEL CULTURE

The impulse to shut down and shut up those who disagree has led to what is called *cancel culture*. Strossen (2020) wrote that

> a free expression culture seeks to further debate and discussion. The opposite is true of cancel culture, which instead seeks to end discussion, or at least to truncate it, by summarily dismissing certain ideas—or even certain speakers— as ineligible for inclusion in the exchange. Accordingly, cancel culture accepts and even encourages conclusory repudiations of arguments and ad hominem attacks on speakers, and does not insist on reasoned analysis or evidence-based

arguments. Cancel culture also uses intimidating tactics, threatening to punish certain speakers through harsh measures, including even outright exile from the university community via expulsion (of students) or firing (of faculty or staff members). (pp. 1–2)

In our highly polarized society, one side often uses the term "cancel culture" to prevent consideration of the other side's ideas, evidence, arguments, and opinions. When it is weaponized and used to silence the other side, hurling the term "cancel culture" is in itself an expression of cancel culture and an attempt to "cancel" the other side. The term then is clearly a false accusation against those trying to encourage rather than shut down speech and open consideration. For example, asking for verifiable evidence when inaccurate, inflammatory, or derogatory bigotries or traditions are invoked or for thoughtful consideration of the impact of words on people who often are members of marginalized populations are clearly *not* attempts to cancel. However, trying to block people from hearing a speaker, shouting down a speaker so they cannot deliver a lecture, or passing laws to ban books on certain topics—however righteous the cause—is cancel culture.

Overcoming cancel culture and its damaging effects is necessary for discussing topics entangled in taboos, silencing, controversies, myths, and dogmas. It is important to speak *openly* and *honestly*, and listen *actively* and *respectfully* to what others—particularly those who disagree—say. We are most likely to learn when we listen patiently, respectfully, and actively, trying to understand the topic as the other person sees it and actively imagining being in their place. Especially when trying to talk about difficult issues, people may speak less than clearly, misstate facts, rely on shaky reasoning, and make a mess of the whole thing. Is it possible to get beyond frustration or anger to focus on the best or most important parts of another's arguments? As Huxley (1893/2011) wrote, "There is no greater mistake than the hasty conclusion that opinions are worthless because they are badly argued" (p. 369).

Authentic discussion of challenging topics may depend on our willingness and ability to negotiate the gulf between some perspectives. Words that are part of our heritage, part of our everyday vocabulary, and essential to speaking honestly and directly about a taboo topic may be strange and difficult to understand for someone with a very different background or perspective. Taboo topics also may be profoundly offensive and insulting or even blasphemous to those who hold certain religious beliefs, or they may come across as threatening. Similarly, people vary widely in how they express themselves nonverbally, particularly about passionate topics. It is important to pay attention to signs that we or others are feeling in any way threatened, afraid, or nervous, a theme explored in more detail in a subsequent section. Consider the following questions:

- Have you or someone you knew been victimized by what you would call cancel culture?
    - What happened?
    - Did it seem fair?
    - What did you learn from the experience?

- Are there topics that you believe should be off-limits in training programs? Why? If someone raised an "off-limits" topic, how would you respond?

- Can you think of anything a professor might say in the normal course of leading a class discussion that, if it were captured on smartphone video and went viral, might lead to an effort—either among students or from the surrounding community—to "cancel" that professor (e.g., get them fired or silenced in some way)?

- Can you think of anything a psychotherapist might ask or say in the ordinary course of psychotherapy that, if it were secretly recorded by the patient and went viral, might lead to an effort to "cancel" the therapist in terms of harassment, filing of ethics and licensing complaints, and so on?

INCREASED PARTISANSHIP AND HYPERPOLARIZATION

Negotiating gulfs between ideas and viewpoints has become much harder with the increasing partisanship and polarization. Hare and Poole (2014) noted that "even the most casual observer of American politics cannot help but notice that partisan conflict has grown sharper, unrelenting, and more ideological over recent decades" (p. 411). They stated the following:

> The study of polarization in contemporary American politics produces unambiguous and important results: The Democratic and Republican parties in Congress are more polarized than at any time since the end of Reconstruction, and a single liberal–conservative dimension explains the vast majority of legislators' vote choices, including on a wide array of social/cultural issues. We are now firmly entrenched in a political era that is characterized by the ubiquity of unidimensional, polarized political conflict. (p. 428)

The increased partisanship and hyperpolarization have brought with them rising hostility and hate. D. F. Stone (2019) documented the rise of hyperpartisan animosity in the United States. Other researchers have suggested it is linked to decreased cognitive flexibility:

> In a sample of over 700 U.S. citizens, partisan extremity was related to lower levels of cognitive flexibility, regardless of political orientation, across 3 independent cognitive assessments of cognitive flexibility. This was evident across multiple statistical analyses, including quadratic regressions, Bayes factor analysis, and interrupted regressions. (Zmigrod et al., 2020, p. 407)

Intense political partisanship and hyperpolarization makes us more likely to dehumanize those we disagree with. Polarization has been linked to dehumanization (Moore-Berg et al., 2020). This tendency is not exclusive to either major U.S. political party. Research by Martherus et al. (2021) found a "pronounced willingness by both Democrats and Republicans to dehumanize members of the out-party" (p. 517).

Negotiating the gulfs that divide specific groups will likely demand the good faith, creativity, flexibility, and ability to adopt and appreciate other perspectives, determination, persistence, emotional intelligence, and humor of all members.

What thoughts and feelings do you have as you consider the following questions?

- In your current training program or work setting, is there any political partisanship of the kind discussed in this section? How, if at all, does it affect what topics are and are not discussed, and how they are discussed?

- In your current or previous training program, was there any partisanship regarding theoretical orientations, methods of assessment, diagnosis, and intervention, or other aspects of the training?
  - For example, was there any partisanship between those teaching and learning cognitive behavioral approaches and those teaching and learning psychodynamic approaches?
  - Or was there complete harmony and mutual respect?
  - Or was there only one approach taught?

- Whatever your politics, assume you have a new client who is a political activist at the extreme other end of the spectrum from you.
  - What challenges, if any, might you experience in providing psychotherapy to this person, perhaps enabling them to become more effective in their political activism?
  - Under what conditions, if any, would you disclose your own political beliefs to the client? Why?

SELF-CENSORSHIP

Many people silence themselves. They censor what they say. Over the years, this tendency to keep our mouths shut about certain topics has grown stronger. In some social settings, this may be appropriate as a matter of respect for others. However, in psychotherapy, all matters must be open for consideration, and keeping secrets or other forms of self-censorship tend to undermine both the relationship and the therapy itself. If the client hides pieces of the problem, what they want out of therapy, or key parts of their history, or if the therapist feels unable to raise these topics, neither is in a good position to make this joint venture work.

J. L. Gibson and Sutherland (2020) described

> the dramatic change in levels of self-censorship over the past 70 or so years. At the height of the 1950s Red Scare, when a circumstantial miscue could land a person in jail, Stouffer . . . reported that only 13.4% of the American people felt less free to "speak their mind" than they used to; fully 84.7% said they did feel free to speak their minds. . . . During an era in which many perhaps *should have been* fearful of speaking their minds, in fact very few Americans seemed to have personally felt [reluctant to speak]. (p. 2)

They reviewed survey data suggesting that from the Red Scare in the 1950s to the present, the percentage of people who report feeling afraid to speak their mind has tripled. They concluded that "public opinion on most matters is slow, perhaps even very slow, to change. But perceptions of the availability of individual-level perceived political freedom changed rather dramatically from 1954 to 2019" (p. 2).

Studies have suggested that a majority of us now fear speaking up. For example,

> a new CATO Institute national survey finds that self-censorship is on the rise in the United States. Nearly two-thirds—62%—of Americans say the political climate these days prevents them from saying things they believe because others might find them offensive. The share of Americans who self-censor has risen several points since 2017 when 58% of Americans agreed with this statement. These fears cross partisan lines. Majorities of Democrats (52%), independents (59%) and Republicans (77%) all agree they have political opinions they are afraid to share. (Ekins, 2020, para. 1)

Consider the following questions:

- In your current or previous psychotherapy training, did you ever want to raise a topic, ask a question, or make a point but ended up censoring yourself?
  - What factor(s) kept you from speaking?
  - What do you think would have happened if you'd spoken up?

- Do you believe there are others in your current or past training program who have not always spoken up freely, honestly, and directly on topics that were important to them?
  - Why do you believe they remained silent?
  - What might have made it easier for them to speak?
- What changes, if any, in training programs might enable them to address issues of self-censorship effectively so that trainees become competent and confident later on as therapists to raise and discuss difficult topics with their clients?

FRIGHTENED ACADEMICS

Parts of the dominant culture have depicted the Ivory Tower as an almost utopian setting (those of you actually in this "utopian setting" can stop laughing) where the free exchange of ideas flourishes in service of developing knowledge. In this popular fantasy, colleges and universities provide separate, safe, and neutral spaces removed from the stresses and strife of the larger society. Academia is viewed as an "alma mater"—a fostering, nourishing, or kind mother.

Anyone who has set foot on campus probably knows these idealistic descriptions often fall far short of reality. Many of them foster a culture of elitism, reinforce the dominant cultural narratives, and are unwelcoming to those challenging the status quo. Members of socially minoritized communities or perspectives that have contradicted dominant cultural constructions have been, and still are, sometimes ignored, demeaned, discriminated against, and silenced (e.g., rarely called on in class, quickly interrupted, their comments ignored). Historically, these groups have included faculty and students that are women; Women of Color; people of low socioeconomic status; working-class people; people with disabilities; and LGBTQIA+ (lesbian, gay, bisexual, transgender, questioning or queer, intersex, asexual, and other forms of sexual and gender identities and orientations) people. These faculty and students continue to find themselves underrepresented, particularly in tenured faculty and upper level administrative positions in which they may face beliefs lacking in validity that they are less capable of intellectual rigor, and they disproportionately encounter other forms of silencing and double standards for success in their positions (e.g., poor student evaluations, complaints; Agathangelou & Ling, 2002; A. M. Jones, 2021; Reyes et al., 2021; Vaccaro, 2017).

Despite academia's persistent image in some circles as offering protection— or "academic freedom"—for the free exchange of ideas, both faculty members and students have never been immune to fear of speaking their minds. McWhorter (2020), for example, reported that

> this year, the Heterodox Academy conducted an internal member survey of 445 academics. "Imagine expressing your views about a controversial issue while at work, at a time when faculty, staff, and/or other colleagues were present. To what extent would you worry about the following consequences?" To the hypothetical "My reputation would be tarnished," 32.68 percent answered "very concerned" and 27.27 percent answered "extremely concerned." To the hypothetical "My career would be hurt," 24.75 percent answered "very concerned" and 28.68 percent answered "extremely concerned." In other words, *more than half the respondents consider expressing views beyond a certain consensus in an academic setting quite dangerous to their career trajectory* [emphasis added]. (para. 6)

According to the Scholars at Risk's (2021) latest annual report, *Free to Think: Report of the Scholars at Risk Academic Freedom Monitoring Project*, these fears are far from groundless. In the section of the report focusing on U.S. colleges and universities, they reported cases of

- disrupting and harassing online events;

- pressures inflicted on individual professors and students from political actors either external to the universities or from university leaders themselves;

- political and legislative attacks that attempt to prohibit the teaching of particular scholarly ideas, theories, or other subject matter; and

- the imposition of travel restrictions, launching of formal investigations, and prosecution of professors and researchers in ways that severely undermine academic freedom for both U.S.–based and international academicians. (pp. 93–97)

Recognizing and addressing fear, apprehension, anxiety, and unease—our own and others—are key to opening up authentic discussion of difficult topics. Doing so may be considered one of the therapist's most important skills and interventions. These feelings may impact multiple facets of life. Some may fear, as mentioned earlier, that saying "the wrong thing" may affect their career and perhaps get them fired or thrown out of school—and it might. Some may worry that challenging the prevailing "givens" may make them less popular—or maybe an outcast—among other students or faculty, which may be true. Some may be the first ones in their family to attend college or graduate school and feel uncomfortable with the setting and speaking up in that environment. Some may be the only person of their race, ethnicity, sexual/affectional orientation, political views, religion, or disability status and be uneasy with their "outsider" status. Some may speak with an accent and have concerns that others will become impatient with them or view them as less than fully American. Some may be undocumented and fear that something they say—or someone believing they should not be in the country—will get them deported. Some may fear that something they say will jeopardize their financial aid or letters of recommendation. The list goes on and on. If we do not deal with our own and others' fear, apprehension, anxiety, and unease in academia, it will block full participation and authentic discussion.

Consider the following questions:

- In your current or past training program, did any trainees or faculty seem uncomfortable or afraid to talk about certain topics, to say the wrong thing, or in some other way to speak openly, honestly, and directly?
  - What were the forbidden topics or "the wrong thing"?
  - How, if at all, was the fear or discomfort dealt with? Was it openly acknowledged and discussed?

- If fear and discomfort are actively ignored or in other ways not addressed effectively in training programs, can you identify ways in which that might affect (a) the training process itself, (b) the therapists who graduate from the program, or (c) how the graduates later talk with clients and conduct psychotherapy?

EDUCATIONAL GAG ORDERS

Educational gag orders restrict what teachers can teach or say. PEN America, an organization devoted to protecting free expression, recently documented and discussed 54 educational gag orders that lawmakers introduced in 24 state legislatures during the first nine months of 2021 alone (Friedman & Tager, 2021). These bills restrict what can be taught or discussed in K–12 schools and higher education. At the time of the report, 11 of the bills had already been enacted and become state law. PEN's analysis identified four major themes:

1. Each of these bills represents an effort to impose content- and viewpoint-based censorship.

2. Individually and collectively, these bills will have a foreseeable chilling effect on the speech of educators and trainers: Even when crafted in ways that nominally permit free expression, they send an unmistakable signal that specific ideas, arguments, theories, and opinions may not be tolerated by the government.

3. These bills are based on a misrepresentation of how intellectual frameworks are taught, and threaten to constrain educators' ability to teach a wide range of subjects.

4. Many of these bills include language that purports to uphold free speech and academic inquiry. This language, intended to help safeguard these bills from legal and constitutional scrutiny, does little or nothing to change the essential nature of these bills as instruments of censorship. (Friedman & Tager, 2021, para. 14)

Banning certain books from schools is a form of an educational gag order, restricting what books a teacher can assign or make available. In an article titled "Book Ban Efforts Are Spreading Across the US," E. A. Harris and Alter (2022) reported on unprecedented efforts to ban books and press criminal charges against school librarians, noting that

> book challenges aren't just coming from the right: "Of Mice and Men" and "To Kill a Mockingbird," for example, . . . were among the library association's 10 most-challenged books in 2020. In the Mukilteo School District in Washington State, the school board voted to remove "To Kill a Mockingbird"—voted the best book of the past 125 years in a survey of readers conducted by *The New York Times Book Review*—from the ninth-grade curriculum at the request of staff members. (para. 21)

One of Texas's new educational gag order laws prompted a district school leader to instruct teachers that any book about the Holocaust must be balanced with opposing views. The new law led teachers in the district to report that they feared they would be punished for making available books addressing racism, slavery, or the Holocaust (Hixenbaugh & Hylton, 2021).

About 3 months later, an Indiana state senator, discussing a bill that would govern what teachers could teach, stated that any teaching about Nazism and fascism must not take a position but must present both sides and be impartial (Peiser, 2022). That same month (January 2022), a school board in Tennessee voted unanimously to ban *The Complete Maus: A Survivor's Tale* (Spiegelman, 1996), the Pulitzer Prize–winning story of the Holocaust (Wegner, 2022). One board member explained that the book attempted to "indoctrinate" children (Harrison, 2022, para. 9).

Calls for a more balanced view of the Holocaust, Nazism, and fascism may be viewed in the context of President Donald J. Trump's arguing to his then chief of staff, former General John Kelly, that "Hitler did a lot of good things" (Bender, 2021, p. 132). He cited, as one example, an improvement in Germany's economy during the 1930s (Graham, 2021).

Consider the following questions:

- Do you believe it is ever appropriate to ban books from psychotherapy training programs? Does that include (a) books that advocate conversion therapy; (b) books asserting, based on the authors' analysis of studies, that there are significant racial differences in intelligence; or (c) marital counseling texts based on religious principles, such as a wife's rightful subservience to her husband and same-sex relationships as sinful?

• If a hypothetical therapist never had exposure to any books about the Holocaust because they were banned from their school, how, if at all, do you think this might affect their ability to work effectively with a Holocaust survivor or the sons or daughters of Holocaust survivors?

It is only when the social context surrounding our work as therapists is taken into account that we can begin to understand, counter, and transcend these formidable barriers to authentic discussions in our professional work. Such contextual factors include a history of psychology and psychotherapy literature, theory, and practice that often have pathologized difference; the failure of the discipline to, until relatively recently, acknowledge its own subjective social positioning in what has been described as social bigotry wrapped in psychological accoutrements; censorship of nondominant cultural narratives and perspectives; hyperpolarization; educational gag orders and the banning of books; and the widespread fear of teaching or saying the wrong thing. The next chapter focuses on how silence and silencing have shaped the psychotherapy profession.

2 A SILENCED PROFESSION
The Toxic Effects of Taboo Topics

As therapists, we face a paradox. We practice talk therapy and encourage our clients to speak freely about even the most private, sensitive, and some-times painful topics. Yet, we may avoid discussing some key issues openly, honestly, and directly. For example, consider the topics discussed in Chapters 7 through 15:

- physical difference and disability
- sexual and affectional orientation
- sexual reactions to clients
- anger
- oppression
- White supremacy culture
- religion
- money and fees
- death and dying

Can you think of instances in your own life when you spoke with less than complete openness and honesty about these topics?

https://doi.org/10.1037/0000350-003
Speaking the Unspoken: Breaking the Silence, Myths, and Taboos That Hurt Therapists and Patients, by K. S. Pope, N. Y. Chavez-Dueñas, H. Y. Adames, J. L. Sonne, and B. A. Greene

When you think of the psychotherapy textbooks you've come across, to what extent are these nine topics adequately covered?

Have the lectures and other formal teachings you've heard on psychotherapy, taken as a whole, discussed these topics in ways that help prepare you to deal with them with clients?

We're going to go out on a limb and predict that most of you have found yourselves at times reluctant to say what's on your mind, what you're really thinking about these topics, and that the psychotherapy texts and lectures on psychotherapy you've encountered have tended to fall short in addressing these topics adequately. Which leads to another question: Why do we therapists suddenly lose our voice?

The profession, politics, or society can impose rules, warning and pushing us away from fully and freely addressing some areas. Chapter 1 discussed how these codes mutated, magnified, and metastasized. Psychotherapy training and practice now take place in a context that includes political polarization, cancel culture, states that legislate what topics cannot be taught in schools and universities, and clashes over valid versus "fake" news. It is difficult to find examples of training that exist in a cultural and political vacuum, completely immune to these forces woven into the context in which we live our lives, are trained, and practice. (Occasionally we may encounter an oasis—a professor or a practicum supervisor—who has struggled against these forces and offers us a chance to explore taboo topics on a deeper level. Have you encountered such opportunities?)

Organizations and institutions not only fall prey in diverse ways to these forces, but they can also cultivate their own cultures that make it unsafe, unwise, or costly to talk freely about taboo topics. Our feelings of uncertainty, insecurity, inferiority, anxiety, competitiveness, perfectionism, fear, shame, guilt, and on and on can lead us to remain silent about certain topics or to wrap them in euphemisms, cliches, abstractions, and other tools for avoiding open, honest, and direct discussion (see Chapter 3).

The silence is not always willful and deliberate. We may not talk about something because we simply don't recognize it's there. It's as if the famous "elephant in the room" is either completely invisible or doing an uncanny impersonation of something else. How can this happen? Therapists may focus on something else with such determination that they don't notice certain other issues or topics. Consider, for example, a new client who walks into the therapist's office. The therapist notices that the client is significantly overweight and begins attributing—before the client can say anything—any problems the client might have to the client's weight and supposed eating disorder. The client may want to explore how they are discriminated against at work because of their weight. But the therapist is trapped in the view that the problem is the client's weight and does not really listen to and understand the client's view. The therapist begins interpreting the client's talk about people at work discriminating against them as both externalization (i.e., the client trying to blame others and avoiding taking responsibility for putting on too much weight) and avoidance (i.e., not accepting what the therapist is convinced is the nature and source of the client's problem). The client ends up feeling unheard and unhelped.

Or perhaps this client's problem is entirely unrelated to weight. Maybe the client wants to talk about feeling that their clergy is being inappropriate to them, or that they are subject to racial discrimination, or that they find themselves suddenly afraid that they will die soon. For the therapist, all such talk is a wasteful detour away from the central problem of weight. No matter what the client says, all roads lead to weight for this therapist. Even if the client begins experiencing a heart attack during the session and anxiously describes the symptoms to the therapist, this therapist might respond, "Have you ever noticed that when I bring up the topic of your weight, you begin experiencing the symptoms of an anxiety attack?"

But therapists can also willfully and deliberately enforce the silence. When someone (e.g., a client, a supervisor, a colleague) breaks the rules and confronts us with a taboo topic we don't want to deal with, we may put our cognitive skills to work, denying that the subject is relevant or essential, or hiding how uncomfortable it makes us feel. We may also put our verbal skills into high gear, interrupting or skating quickly past (or over) the topic, or discounting the person who broke the silence. Or we may instantly redefine what they are saying and deflect to safer ground. If all else fails, we can discredit the speaker while ignoring what they said. As an example, imagine that during a staff meeting, the only Therapist of Color raises the topic of White supremacy culture and how it affects hiring and promotions, how clinic clients are diagnosed and treated, and how staff meetings are conducted. Perhaps the other people in the meeting chime in at the same time, trying to make the following points:

- "There really isn't adequate time left in this meeting to discuss such a complex topic."

- "That topic was not on the agenda."

- "There are other more pressing topics—such as glitches in the new electronic record program, the upcoming state's inspection, and the shortage of neuropsychological assessment materials—that must be addressed first."

- "Why is there so much criticism and emphasis on the negative? Can't we talk about and give ourselves credit for all the ways the clinic has improved and everything we've accomplished despite all the challenges? You know, it's really easy to find flaws if you look hard enough, and that's all you're looking for."

- "Who are you accusing, and why are you playing the race card?"

TWO HISTORICAL EXAMPLES

The introduction emphasized the value of learning and considering the history of the field. In this chapter, we presented examples of how issues of great significance fell prey to the mechanisms of silencing, denial, discounting, and distortions that we discuss in this book, and how the field overcame—at least in part—these mechanisms and can now recognize, appreciate, and speak more directly about these issues. This history gives us an understanding of how profoundly a topic can be blocked from view, how this happens, and how we can overcome that barrier. It also invites us to reflect on how that process may be playing out with other topics today. What issues are we missing? What issues do we dismiss as insignificant? What issues do we completely misinterpret? This history also can help us grasp just how harmful this silence—and the myths and unspoken rules associated with it—can be to psychotherapy patients. Take, for example, the decades of silence about incest and rape. Mental health professionals tended to assume that actual cases of incest were so rare as to be virtually nonexistent. Freud (1917/1965) wrote,

> Almost all of my women patients told me that they had been seduced by their father. I was driven to recognize in the end that these reports were untrue and so came to understand that the hysterical symptoms are derived from phantasies and not from real occurrences. (p. 120)

Freud taught that when girls say that their father imposed some form of sexual contact with them, it could always be safely assumed that this false accusation represented a fantasy.

Many subsequent works did not adopt Freud's psychoanalytic framework but still agreed that actual incest was so rare that most clinicians would never encounter it in practice. For example, Weinberg's 1955 book, *Incest Behavior*, claimed that the best evidence showed that only one or two cases of incest might occur for every million people. Twenty years later, the authoritative *Comprehensive Textbook of Psychiatry* estimated the incidence of incest at somewhere between 1.1 and 1.9 per million (Henderson, 1975). Herman (1981) documented in detail the difficulties clinicians, researchers, and society more generally had in recognizing the reality of incest, breaking the collective silence, and dispelling the myths in that area.

The hush surrounding rape—like the silence surrounding incest—also reflected the myth that it tended to be women's fantasy about an innocent man and that it very rarely actually occurred. Amir (1971) could not find any book focused entirely on the topic of rape. Estrich (1987) noted that at least up to the early 1970s, rape accusations were widely viewed as "lies or fantasies" (p. 43).

Wigmore's (1934/1970) authoritative text on legal evidence shows the degree to which both the psychiatric and legal professions, even as late as 1970, held the view that virtually all claims of rape were false and simply reflected an inherent tendency of women to fantasize about being raped and to make false accusations. *Evidence in Trials at Common Law* stated authoritatively that

> chastity may have a direct connection with veracity, viz. when a woman or young girl testifies as complainant against a man charged with a sexual crime-rape, rape under age, seduction, assault. Modern psychiatrists have amply studied . . . girls and women coming before the courts in all sorts of cases. Their psychic complexes are multifarious, distorted partly by inherent defects, partly by diseased derangements or abnormal instincts, partly by bad social environment, partly by temporary physiological or emotional conditions. . . . The unchaste (let us call It) mentality finds incidental but direct expression in the narration of imaginary sex-incidents of which the narrator is the heroine or the victim. . . . No judge should ever let a sex offense go to the jury unless the female complainant's social history and mental makeup have been examined and testified to by a qualified physician. . . . The reason I think that rape in particular belongs in this category is one well known to psychologists, namely, that fantasies of being raped are exceedingly common in women, indeed one may almost say that they are probably universal. (pp. 745–746)

TOXIC EFFECTS OF SILENCE

These examples suggest the harm that can occur when we fail to recognize and talk frankly, realistically, and thoroughly about critical issues. For instance, countless girls and women who found the courage to report being sexually abused by their fathers or raped by someone were reflexively dismissed as describing their fantasies or false memories of events that never happened. As a result, incest and rapes could continue. The sex abusers and rapists were not held responsible and were free to assault other children, women, and men sexually. Victims found no support, protection, legal validation, justice, or appropriate social and mental health services.

Further, the training of future psychotherapists suffers if instructors and supervisors perpetuate the silence surrounding taboo topics in their education of trainees. A recent study examined early career psychologists' inquiries regarding their clients' sexual abuse histories (Nixon & Quinlan, 2022). A significant majority reported that they did not routinely ask such questions. They indicated that their training in sexual abuse was inadequate, leaving them unsure of what to do, uncomfortable with the topic, and worried about stigma and adverse outcomes.

Research further underscores the importance for clients and the therapy itself of the therapists' interest and engagement in discussing sensitive topics. For example, in analogue studies with Clients of Color, therapists who addressed cultural issues (e.g., a White client's anger at People of Color's seeming to "take advantage" of affirmative action, a Black client's discomfort about having taken part in a protest that became violent) appeared to facilitate positive client outcomes (including more intimate client self-disclosures). And, conversely, those who avoided discussions with racial content evoked frustration with the therapist (Knox et al., 2003). In another study of actual therapists and clients in a university counseling center, clients who perceived that their therapist missed opportunities to discuss their cultural identity reported worse therapy outcomes (Owen et al., 2016). Further, using a similar real-life sample, Owen et al. (2017) found that therapists' comfort with addressing cultural issues was associated with racial/ethnic differences in clients' decisions to stop therapy.

The silence also hurts psychotherapists. When topics become taboo, classroom professors, clinical supervisors, and other educators tend to (a) skip right over them, (b) give them only cursory attention, (c) distract, or (d) even actively discourage discussion should someone dare to bring a topic up. New generations of psychotherapists inherit these codes of silence and move into practice with a lack of awareness, knowledge, or skills to respond when these topics emerge in their work with clients (S. M. Harris & Hays, 2008). Instead, therapists tend to experience anxiety, discomfort, confusion, freezing, hurt, sadness, offense, or anger when clients "break the code" by bringing an unspoken topic into the session (Ahn et al., 2020; Cross, 1991; Pope et al., 1986; Pope & Tabachnick, 1993). Therapists may then be at a loss for an empathic nonjudgmental response; fall silent; change the topic; say something unintentionally hurtful; or plow on with an undermining, counterproductive intervention (Ahn et al., 2020). The therapeutic alliance is at risk of rupture, and the therapy process is at risk of stalling or withering (Muran et al., 2009). As the therapy falters or fails, therapists may feel embarrassed, guilty, ineffective, and incompetent—and the cycle of silence continues and strengthens.

To overcome the silence effectively, we need to understand systems of silencing and the cognitive cues for keeping quiet, the topics of the next chapter. Let's get started.

3 SYSTEMS OF SILENCING AND COGNITIVE CUES FOR KEEPING QUIET

We live our lives, pursue our education, and carry out our work as therapists and supervisors in a complex network of formal and informal social systems. These organizations include our families, social networks, religious or spiritual groups, political groups, governmental institutions, universities, clinical training sites, and workplaces. Our contact with the people in these systems may be through face-to-face encounters, Zoom and other video conferencing (which became much more prevalent with the onset of the COVID-19 pandemic), telephone, social media (e.g., Facebook, Instagram, Twitter, KakaoTalk, WhatsApp, Messenger, Viber, TikTok, Weixin, WeChat, Snapchat), internet lists, and other new and evolving means of communication.

Whenever we set foot—literally or virtually—into almost any organization, we pick up cues and clues about what we are encouraged to notice and what we are supposed to ignore. We start to pick up on what topics are allowed or favored, which can bring unease, fear, anger, disapproval, or even reprisals if mentioned. It is hard—perhaps impossible—to find an organization that lacks these implicit rules guiding what we can and can't say. Every organization guards its image and its secrets. All organizations have their taboo topics or things best left unsaid.

https://doi.org/10.1037/0000350-004
Speaking the Unspoken: Breaking the Silence, Myths, and Taboos That Hurt Therapists and Patients, by K. S. Pope, N. Y. Chavez-Dueñas, H. Y. Adames, J. L. Sonne, and B. A. Greene

Each organization has its preferred ways of communicating these implicit rules, emphasizing how important each one is, including how severe the consequences of breaking a given rule will be. These rules may not have evolved from any base motives and may even have been unintended consequences of how the organization tried to reach worthy goals. They may have become so internalized that longtime members of the organization may be unaware that they are enforcing these rules.

This chapter is a brief reminder of how frequently we encounter—often without noticing—the rules, secrets, and taboos in organizations, including those in which psychotherapy is taught and practiced. And when such unspoken expectations undermine an individual's values or the stated values, purpose, and goals of the organization, the weight of those expectations can, in turn, influence individuals' roles in following, strengthening, or challenging them.

SYSTEMS OF SILENCING

The influence of unspoken rules can remain a distant abstraction until we see how they work in our own lives. As you think about the various organizations—educational, business, clinical, religious, political, professional, social, or your own family—you've been a member of, consider the following questions:

- What were some messages conveyed about topics that were okay and not okay to bring up (i.e., taboo topics)?

- As you think about these messages, were they explicitly or implicitly conveyed?

- Were the messages conveyed to everyone?
  - If not, were there certain individuals or groups of people to whom the messages did not apply?
  - Who could get away with breaking or discussing unspoken topics without suffering significant consequences?

- Did any of the messages seem to have a detrimental effect on the organization's values, purpose, or goals?

- Did any of the messages seem to have a detrimental effect on individuals inside or outside the organization?

- Did any of these messages seem to have a detrimental effect on you?

- How did you learn what the messages were?

- Did anyone discuss or complain about the messages privately? Did you?

- Did you ever consider challenging, breaking, or at least trying to bring up a topic that was considered taboo? What factors led to your consideration?

- Did anyone else ever challenge, break, or try to discuss a taboo topic? If so, what happened?

- Did you ever challenge, break, or try to bring up a taboo topic? If so, what happened?

FACTORS INFLUENCING OUR INDIVIDUAL CHOICES TO STAY SILENT

Organizations cultivate, communicate, and enforce their silencing systems, but each of us chooses to avoid taboo topics or risk speaking up. When we consider opening our mouths to engage in risky speech, we must confront our internal voices urging us to reconsider. These inner voices can point out the benefits of keeping quiet and the costs of violating taboos.

Consider the critical components of self-silencing systems that can affect our intentions or decisions to speak up in graduate school, our first real start in learning about and gaining skills in our profession. The habits and patterns we learn in graduate school will likely influence our later behavior as professionals. Many of our patterns of self-silencing get their start in early family and social experiences and are reinforced in graduate school. Did you ever decide not to speak up in graduate school because of any of the factors described next in this section? Which factors do you find personally compelling when you're even just considering speaking up? Are there other factors not listed here that contribute to your silence?

Rules and Lessons Learned Early

We are educated in our families and early social interactions. We internalize the social systems of silent rules into personal systems of self-silencing. For example, those in the majority are taught "lessons" and "rules" about diverse "others" that may not be spoken, much less questioned. And those with diverse identities who have experienced oppression, such as members of racially or sexually minoritized communities, are likely to quickly recognize silencing messages and understand the cost associated when tempted to disrupt silencing messages by raising topics that may shake the status quo.

Other social rules are carefully taught. For example, we may have been instructed early on to "ignore" another's physical difference or disability. Or we may have been warned that our experience of sexual attraction or anger, much less the expression of either, is inappropriate. Or we may have been admonished not to speak of another's serious illness or impending death. And, often, these lessons are offered differentially depending on our gender, our sexual and affectional orientation, our religion, or our culture or ethnicity.

We bring these internalized social lessons and rules with us into graduate school and then into the workplace. And as discussed next, graduate school, clinical training sites, and clinical practices are also social, institutional structures that may not naturally foster recognition and exploration of taboo topics.

Competition

Graduate schools can, whether or not intentionally, encourage competition. We compete to get into a graduate school. Especially if the grading is on the curve, we compete for grades. We compete for the professors' time, attention, approval, teaching and research assistantships, and letters of recommendation. If resources are scarce, we compete for financial support, grants, and other resources. In many organizations, those who tend to be positively evaluated, promoted, and succeed are people who steer clear of the taboos, stick to the unspoken rules, and fit themselves to match institutional expectations (Asaoka, 2020; Detert & Treviño, 2010; Jackall, 1988; see Chapter 27 in Pope et al., 2021).

Conservation of Energy

Grad school is—to put it mildly—a demanding experience. Unless we start the process already knowing everything the professors plan to teach and possess the skills we're supposedly there to learn, we have to work hard, step outside our comfort zones, and experience failures and frustrations along with successes. Some of us need to hold down one or more part-time jobs to pay the bills. Some have family responsibilities. Some try to maintain a personal life, have some fun and relax. And there are rumors that some students even try to get enough exercise and sleep. Why spend additional time and energy going against the institutional culture by speaking up and opening (a) doors marked "secret," (b) a Pandora's box, or (c) a can of worms (Pope, 2017)? Isn't that energy better spent reading the assignment posted for the week? Or on preparing for the next exam, working on that dissertation, applying to clinical training sites, studying for comps, or telling your professors once again just how much you've always admired them and their work?

As a working professional, you have many competing demands, including teaching classes; seeing clients; supervising trainees, interns, or postdocs; consulting; completing paperwork; and balancing your job with your personal life. Making waves by raising topics that are known to be silenced within your institution can be an additional form of labor that can be both physically, emotionally, and sometimes even spiritually exhausting. You may decide that the potential to create change by discussing taboo topics is not worth your time and energy.

Risk Avoidance

Money, sex abuse, racism, and oppression are examples of topics that prior generations of therapists seemed unable to discuss in what we view as an open, realistic, fact-based way. But even these days, it can be challenging to talk openly about these topics, even in otherwise supportive graduate training programs. Some students may want to share their thoughts and feelings on a range of issues regarding fees and payment for services, including

- the amount they want to charge for therapy,

- whether they want to provide treatment to wealthy people who willing to pay out of pocket so they can charge high fees and not have to deal with insurance claims,

- prior authorizations for needed treatment,

- coverage limits,

- "lost" forms, or

- delayed or partial payments.

Other students may want to share some of their personal history of having been sexually assaulted or abused to inform a discussion of those issues. Students of Color may want to talk about how White supremacy culture impacts their lives. Perhaps they may bring up the lack of training on addressing topics of oppression in clinical practice and how such shortcomings may affect their future careers. However, to speak up honestly and openly about these topics risks being judged and stereotyped by their instructors, supervisors, and fellow students in ways that, however subtle and unspoken, may be both influential and hard to shake.

If taboo topics were not addressed in our graduate training, we might feel ill-prepared to manage them as professionals. The lack of preparation and practice is often reflected in our unwillingness to risk raising these topics in our professional roles. In addition, we then inadvertently reinforce the same risk avoidance around uncomfortable, taboo topics that we experienced in our graduate training. Therefore, when students or clients need or want to bring taboo topics into their classes, supervision, or therapy sessions, they may feel apprehensive about the risk and decide not to talk about them. In this way, avoiding taboo topics begins in our graduate training and becomes a vicious cycle of risk avoidance that is difficult to break.

Momentum

If we're doing well—or at least okay—in graduate school, why spoil it? Isn't it better to show respect for the culture of the graduate setting, avoid violating norms, venturing into forbidden territory, or opening a Pandora's box of unpredictable disruption? Why not maintain this wonderful momentum of doing well, observe the institutional guardrails, and try not to jump the tracks? Why not be a team player? Once we've safely graduated, we can always become positive, valuable, speak-the-truth troublemakers and disruptors. Okay, make that once we've gotten licensed—no use sabotaging ourselves and our careers until we've reached the entry ticket to do therapy. *Then* we speak up. Definitely.

But hold on! We have to get a job first. What good are a graduate degree and license—and all the work, time, and money that went into them—if we doom our chances to find employment, put the degree and license to work, start practicing our profession, and actually earn some money? We hold off until we land that job and establish ourselves, and *then* we . . . .

Well, there's no use being stupid about the whole thing: Wouldn't it be wiser to hold off saying or doing anything that would slow our momentum toward a raise; a promotion; an award; or a new, more desirable position with another organization?

Perhaps once safely retired, we might consider . . . .

A Minority of One

At times, we may see things differently from everyone else. Everyone else considers a conclusion logical; we see it as invalid. They know a selection process is fair; we see it as biased or perhaps even racist. They see a factor as irrelevant; we see it as essential. What do we do when we are alone in how we see things? Do we speak up and voice views out of sync with everyone else's? An iconic study from the 1950s offers some interesting data.

In his classic experiment, Solomon Asch (1956) described the basic setup:

> A group of seven to nine individuals was gathered in a classroom to take part in what appeared to be a simple experiment in visual discrimination. They were instructed to match the length of a given line—the standard—with one of

three other lines. One of the three comparison lines was equal to the standard; the other two lengths differed from the standard (and from each other) by considerable amounts. . . . The individuals were instructed to announce their judgments publicly in the order in which they were seated. (p. 3)

Each person who participated in the experiment was not informed that it had been arranged in advance for them to announce their judgments last after the other people had spoken. They also were not informed that the others in the room were confederates who were all instructed to identify the same wrong line as the one that matched the standard. Asch reported that when everyone else announced a clearly wrong answer, about a third (37%) of the participants went along with the crowd and gave the same wrong answer even though they could easily see the correct answer with their own eyes. Participants later, during an interview, described some of their thoughts and feelings as a minority of one.

It's worth taking a moment now to reflect on whether we had some version of these responses when we were in the minority. Consider, too, whether these thoughts and feelings led us to keep quiet, maintain the status quo, and go along with the majority view (see Exhibit 3.1 for a sample of minority-of-one statements from the Asch, 1956, experiment).

Identifying unspoken messages, secrets, and taboos in an organization and maintaining awareness of the factors—especially our personal systems of self-silencing—that influence our individual choices about how to respond are key to learning, growth, and informed practice. This ability is like a muscle: If we train and exercise it, it grows more robust, resilient, and adept. If we neglect it, it withers. The information and exercises in this book focus on strengthening, extending, and enhancing this ability. The next chapter explores the ways in which these factors blocked and warped recognition, exploration, and understanding of a challenging topic: therapists' sexual attractions, arousals, and fantasies.

EXHIBIT 3.1. Minority-of-One Reflective Statements From the Asch (1956) Experiment

I felt like a silly fool.

A question of being a misfit.

I felt they'd think I was a wet blanket or sore thumb.

Some kind of pressure builds up in you. On the first one, I almost started to say something different but afterward, I more or less fell in with them.

It made me seem weak-eyed or weak-headed, like a black sheep.

I began to question whether my own perception was as acute as it seemed to be.

I tried to make myself see it as equal.

I guess my answers tried to minimize my disagreement.

It reminded me of a time when, as a child, my mother threw a cupful of water at me because I couldn't stop crying. My sister was there, and everyone seemed against me; I was separated.

Often mine still looked best, but I figured they were right.

I had a tendency to feel that perhaps I was wrong and might just as well agree with them. As disagreement continued it looked as if I was differing either to show off, to be an individual, or trying to stand out. I did not like that.

I thought that they might have been seeing an optical illusion that I didn't.

After I became a conformist I was mad at myself.

Wish I'd had the guts.

I felt the need to conform. . . . Mob psychology builds upon you. It was more pleasant to agree than to disagree.

The group didn't make me feel bad; I just wanted to agree.

I made my own judgment, then considered the group's judgment, gave it, and regretted it.

I was beginning to become confused and was more prone to their influence.

At first, I thought I was right, then I became convinced the other seven couldn't be wrong. I stayed steady then. Toward the end I lost hope they'd come back to me, and it was too much for coincidence. Became sure I was wrong.

I was disgusted with myself for changing and almost asked for another chance at it.

It is not pleasant to be the only one different.

4 AN EXAMPLE OF THE PROBLEM

Therapists' Sexual Attractions, Arousals, and Fantasies

The problem of the unspoken in organizations, schools, and therapy was outlined in the first three chapters. Chapter 1 presented the problem of silence, myths, and unspoken rules, and outlined the current sociopolitical context in which the problem flourishes. Chapter 2 described how the problem afflicts the field and those who work within it, and how it emerges in our training, our professional organizations, and work as therapists in ways that often hurt our patients, ourselves, and our profession. Chapter 3 focused on the systems of silencing and cues for keeping quiet.

This chapter looks at these factors and forces at work in a major example of the problem: therapists' sexual experiences in therapy, including sexual attraction, sexual arousal, and sexual fantasies about patients. The chapter also presents a detailed and deep dive into the history of this topic. This information will enable a better, more complete, and more informed understanding of therapists' sexual attractions, arousals, and fantasies in their full historical context, showing specific ways the profession dodged, denied, dismissed, and distorted a basic set of experiences shared by most therapists.

https://doi.org/10.1037/0000350-005
Speaking the Unspoken: Breaking the Silence, Myths, and Taboos That Hurt Therapists and Patients, by K. S. Pope, N. Y. Chavez-Dueñas, H. Y. Adames, J. L. Sonne, and B. A. Greene

Readers are encouraged to engage with two sets of questions as they read this history:

- First, does the profession's history of finding ways to ignore, avoid, or remain silent about therapists' sexual attractions, arousals, and fantasies seem securely left behind, a thing of the past?
  - Can you think of ways the profession and its training programs, texts, and practitioners have difficulty fully acknowledging these topics and speaking about them openly, honestly, and directly?

If so, what effect is this "continuing history" having?

- Second, can you think of other aspects of therapy training and practice in which these mechanisms of avoidance and silencing are at work?
  - Assuming you can think of some—unfortunately, there's no shortage— do the mechanisms seem to work differently than they do in regard to therapists' sexual feelings?
  - For each of the different aspects of therapy training and practice that you can think of, what reasons are there for this particular topic area to be off limits?

Despite much progress, which is outlined in this chapter, how we therapists experience and respond to sexual feelings about our patients continues to plague the profession (Alpert et al., 2021; L. S. Brown & Courtois, 2021; Clark & Bennett, 2021; Gómez et al., 2021; Pope et al., 2021; Wenzel, 2021). The reluctance and sometimes fierce resistance to frankly acknowledge these attractions, arousals, and fantasies have been deeply ingrained in the profession's history. Studies starting as early as the 1980s suggest that many graduate training programs and internships have tended to stop short of addressing this issue directly and adequately. Current professional consensus is that the majority of mental health trainees are still not receiving adequate or quality instruction or guidance about the therapist's sexual attractions, arousals, and fantasies (as a topic different from the ethical, legal, and clinical issues involved in actual therapist sexual misconduct; Shelton, 2020; see also Pope et al., 2021).

SOURCES OF DENIAL AND AVOIDANCE

Why do sexual attractions, arousals, and fantasies experienced by therapists and therapists-in-training provoke widespread and long-standing avoidance? In this section, we explore seven possible reasons adapted from Pope (1994) and Pope et al. (2021).

Topics May Be Avoided Because They Are Associated With Sexual Misconduct

Therapists may avoid the topic of sexual feelings and fantasies about patients because of the close association with actual therapists' sexual misconduct with clients. And historically, mental health professions have demonstrated great resistance to acknowledging, much less exploring, reports of violations of the centuries-old prohibition against engaging in sexual involvement with patients.

Psychiatrist Clay Dahlberg (1970), for example, who was finally able to publish his article "Sexual Contact Between Patient and Therapist," described the string of editorial rejections that met his attempts to find a publication outlet. He stated, "I have had trouble getting this paper accepted. . . . I was told that it was too controversial. What a word for a profession which talked about infantile sexuality and incest in Victorian times" (p. 107).

Seven years later, there was still so little published on the topic that Davidson (1977) referred to it as the "Problem With No Name" in the title of her article. More than a decade after that, Gechtman (1989) presented and discussed evidence that resistance to publishing information about social workers who become sexually involved with their clients remained strong among prominent social work associations.

Firm resistance also blocked early research efforts. Published accounts suggest at least two attempts made before 1970 to gather and distribute incidence data on therapist–patient sexual involvement. Shepard (1971) described the reaction that psychologist Harold Greenwald received when he suggested, at a meeting of a clinical psychological association in the 1960s, that the association support research into the occurrence of sexual intimacies between therapists and their patients:

> I just raised the questions . . . intending, as a clinical psychologist, that it be studied like any other phenomenon. And just for raising the question, some members circulated a petition that I should be expelled from the Psychological Association. (Greenwald, as quoted by Shepard, p. 2)

One of the authors of this book verified with Greenwald his account:

> Understand that I was only suggesting that we conduct some research, perhaps a survey, on the subject. All I asked was that we take a look at the topic, that we get some data. But there was talk among some members of expelling me. And they cancelled a radio interview. Because I had been scheduled to speak at the convention, those in charge had arranged for one of the radio stations to interview me at the end of the convention. But when they heard what I said, they told me that they had cancelled my interview, that I would not be one of those invited to the scheduled interviews. It was all very strange, but you could see what a nerve this had touched. There was considerable resistance to airing this topic in public. (H. Greenwald, personal communication, October 1992)

Another psychologist, Bertram Forer, also attempted to encourage the study of therapist–patient sexual intimacies in the late 1960s. Obtaining the approval of the Los Angeles County Psychological Association (LACPA) to conduct a formal survey of their memberships, Forer started the first systematic research into the frequency with which therapists engage in sex with their patients. Unfortunately, his findings indicated a higher rate of sexual intimacies than the research sponsorship had anticipated. On October 28, 1968, the LACPA board of directors, after discussing the research data with the association's leadership, resolved to prohibit the presentation of the findings in any public forum (e.g., convention presentation, journal publication) because it was "not in the best interests of psychology to present it publicly" (B. Forer, personal communication, January 27, 1993; see also Forer, 1980).

Although the Forer data were not permitted to be presented publicly for many years, only a few years later, the first article addressing therapist–patient "sexual improprieties" based on systematically collected empirical data was published. This *American Psychologist* article (Brownfain, 1971) presented an analysis and discussion of 10 years of data about professional liability lawsuits filed against psychologists. The database comprised records maintained by the insurance carrier that provided liability insurance to American Psychological Association (APA) members. Interestingly, this article did not mention any valid complaint involving a psychologist who had actually engaged in sexual intimacies with a patient. Instead, the insurance data were used as the basis for the conclusion:

> The greatest number of [all malpractice] actions are brought by women who lead lives of very quiet desperation, who form close attachments to their therapists, who feel rejected or spurned when they discover that relations are maintained on a formal and professional level, and who then react with allegations of sexual improprieties. (Brownfain, 1971, p. 651)

This period reaching into the early 1970s suggests there may have been considerable resistance in the profession to openly acknowledging and studying violations of the prohibition against therapist–patient sexual involvement. It was not until 1973 that the first survey providing evidence—based on anonymous self-reports of mental health professionals—of sexual contact between therapist and patient was published (Kardiner et al., 1973). And it was not until 1983 and 1984 that the first studies were published that provided evidence of the harm that can result from those violations (Bouhoutsos et al., 1983; Feldman-Summers & Jones, 1984).

Perhaps some of this resistance was based on therapists' sense of shame and embarrassment for the profession that sexual involvements between therapists and patients were happening in the field. A foundational goal of our profession is to help people. It invites the general trust of the public and the specific people who come to us as patients. Many therapists may find it acutely uncomfortable for it to be made public that members of the profession are exploiting the trust of some patients. Public reports of research or other evidence that some therapists sexually use their patients may be seen by some as giving the profession "a bad rep."

The second source of resistance may be that therapists may experience discomfort when the examination of the topic of sexual involvements with patients turns to a focus on individual practitioners. When Harvard University professor Nanette Gartrell and her colleagues planned an anonymous survey of the membership of the American Psychiatric Association to gather information about psychiatrists' attitudes, beliefs, and behavior regarding sexual involvements with patients in the association, the association refused to support the research. There appeared to be a stark contrast between the detailed interest taken in eliciting information from and about patients in this area—about victimized patients' possible "promiscuity," sexual history, predisposing clinical conditions, problems setting limits, and so on—and the American Psychiatric Association's lack of support for an anonymous survey of its membership. As the (then) chair of the Ethics Committee of the American Psychiatric Association explained, "The association does not believe in asking members for 'sensitive information about themselves'" (Bass, 1989, p. 28). Feeling that one's privacy has been invaded—that the spotlight has shifted from the patient's disorders, distress, and actions to include unflattering characteristics and exploitive behaviors of the therapist—may make many therapists uncomfortable.

Perhaps fear of lawsuits also fueled the resistance. Research exploring the occurrence and consequences of therapist–patient sex drew the public's attention to the topic and might have been seen as inviting groundless malpractice suits. One chair of the then American Psychological Association Insurance Trust expressed this fear, stating that "consumers recognize the vulnerability of the provider and are attempting to exploit that vulnerability for 'economic gain'" (Wright, 1985, p. 114).

Another source of resistance may have been a more general concern about economic loss. Therapists likely worried that the loss of public trust in the profession, as cases of therapist–patient sexual involvements were publicized, would cause a decrease in the number of people seeking therapy. Professionals also were concerned that their professional liability insurance premiums would drastically increase. Indeed, increased publication of research on therapist–patient sexual involvement was positively correlated (which, of course, may or may not reflect causation) with an increase in the malpractice suits filed against therapists. During the late 1980s, costs associated with therapist–patient sex claims accounted for about half of all monies paid for claims against psychologists covered by the American Professional Agency insurance carrier, according to the company's president (R. Imbert, personal communication, April 18, 1988). Faced with such actual and potential economic losses, it would not be surprising if therapists were uncomfortable with the topic and ambivalent toward continuing publication of research data that would draw increasing public attention to the topic.

Although the economic concerns may have potentially affected virtually any therapist, they may have been especially acute for members of the American Psychiatric Association, whose organization had a more direct link to the insurance carrier. Alan Stone (A. A. Stone, 1990), professor of psychiatry and law at Harvard and a former president of the American Psychiatric Association, emphasized that

> we should all realize that there is a serious conflict of interest between APA's [American Psychiatric Association's] professional concerns for the victims of sexual exploitation in therapy and its financial concerns when the association's economic interests are at serious risk. (p. 26)

He noted that actions taken to eliminate or cap the coverage for sex claims in professional liability policies seemed to violate the profession's commitment to the welfare of its patients:

> Each of us contributes by paying liability insurance to a fund that has two functions: to protect us and to compensate those who are unfortunate victims of our negligence. With this in mind, the policy decision to exclude victims of sexual exploitation, who are typically women, from participation in our victim compensation fund is difficult to defend. If we are concerned about them, why should they be "victimized" by the exclusion? (A. A. Stone, 1990, p. 25)

The profoundly and understandably adverse professional reactions to sexual exploitation of patients, the resistance raised, and the silences imposed may have become associated with sexual feelings about and reactions to the patient. As a result, these topics became even more difficult to acknowledge and address openly.

The Topic of Sexual Reactions to Clients Is Sensitive and Difficult to Discuss

Sexual feelings, arousals, and fantasies are among the most sensitive topics for anyone to discuss. We learn rules from our families, religious institutions, and cultural systems that silence talk about our sexual experiences. Therapists are no different. Becoming a professional therapist does not suddenly lift those internalized censors and the discomfort that ensues.

Some additional discomfort for mental health professionals around the topic of sexual feelings about patients may be that it brings attention to aspects of the therapist that may seem discordant with the persona of the therapist (in the therapist's own eyes, in the eyes of significant others, in the public's eyes) as a caring provider of help to those who are in need. Therapists may feel legitimate pride in their altruism and the services they provide to those who are hurting. The idea that this altruistic helper may become sexually aroused in the presence of a vulnerable patient may be surprising, alarming, and scary to the therapist, the patient, other professionals, and the general public (Capawana & Walla, 2016).

Studies have shown that some therapists have also come to believe (falsely) that such sexual attractions are unethical (e.g., Nickell et al., 1995; Pope et al., 1986). Therapists and therapists-in-training may feel uncomfortable about self-disclosure of sexual feelings because they are afraid they will be criticized or sanctioned or that their disclosures will be viewed as signs of perversion or inadequacy (or even unsuitability) as a therapist. Even senior and prominent clinicians have found it difficult to disclose their sexual reactions to patients, including Harold Searles (1959). Discussing such reactions, Searles confessed, "I reacted to such feelings with considerable anxiety, guilt, and embarrassment" (p. 183). Indeed, recent research using focus groups found that therapists' fear of others' negative reactions to their disclosure of sexual attraction (i.e., the absence of a "safe environment") was a significant impeding factor contributing to their hesitancy to disclose their feelings to peers and supervisors (Vesentini et al., 2021).

Publishing on the Topic Will Invite Uncomfortable Questions, Disclosures, and Behaviors From Patients

Therapists may be apprehensive that clients may read published research or popular press regarding sexual feelings in psychotherapy (increasingly more likely with the internet) and then ask questions in session about their therapist's feelings of attraction to them, or disclose their own feelings toward the therapist, or even begin enacting romantic or sexualized behaviors toward the therapist. Research findings indicate that such occurrences do happen, and when they do, they evoke feelings of caution, anxiety, fear, and vulnerability in the therapist (Pope et al., 2021; Sonne & Jochai, 2014).

Fear That Discussing the Topic Will Increase the Likelihood of Therapists' Acting Out Their Sexual Feelings

Therapists may fear that openly acknowledging and publishing works on sexual attraction to patients may somehow increase the likelihood that therapists will engage in sex with patients, either in their own work or more generally among all therapists. The premise seems to be that if one begins thinking about the forbidden attraction, it will take root, gain force, and thrive, perhaps achieving an uncontrollable life of its own and eventual expression through action.

To counter this threat, many therapists attempt to drive the reaction from awareness, deny it a foothold in their thoughts and daydreams, and distract attention from it. But the assumption that trying to ignore and block out sexual feelings will produce the best results for therapists, patients, or the profession is likely no more sound than the discredited fallacy that one should never talk about suicide with a patient because bringing up the topic may "plant the seed" in a person who previously had no suicidal ideation and may overwhelm the patient and thus increase the risk that they will die by suicide.

Material on the Topic Will Be Taken Out of Context

Therapists may be concerned that material on therapists' sexual feelings may be misused, misconstrued, taken out of context, and met with intolerance and a lack of objectivity. Freud's attempts to discuss sexual material in the context of psychotherapy met with a flood of misunderstanding, distortions, and resistance not only among the public but also among many of his professional colleagues. E. E. Jones (1961) quoted Freud's dismayed reaction to his experience of attempting to discuss his sexual theories at a meeting of the Vienna Neurological Society:

> I treated my discoveries as ordinary contributions to science and hoped to be met in the same spirit. But the silence with which my addresses were received, the void which formed itself about me, the insinuations that found their way to me, caused me gradually to realize that one cannot count upon views about the part played by sexuality. . . meeting with the same reception as other communications. . . . I could not reckon upon objectivity and tolerance. (p. 177)

The reaction to Freud's ideas about sexuality stands as such a vivid scene in the history of psychotherapy that it may be difficult to escape entirely lingering fears that some versions of the scene may be repeated whenever new areas of sexual exploration are opened up.

Therapists Are (Still) Not Well Trained on the Topic

As noted earlier in the chapter, research suggests that the topic of sexual reactions to patients has been seriously neglected historically in most graduate schools and internships. Graduate training and continuing education on the subject have been deemed important by leaders and trainees in the profession and have increased (Sonne & Jochai, 2014). However, unfortunately, they are not required; are of uneven content, format, and quality; are often rated as inadequate by therapists in practice; and are rarely formally evaluated (Shelton, 2020).

Clearly, the prospect of sexual reactions to patients becoming the focus of discussion in the classroom or in supervision may evoke feelings of discomfort, as described earlier, for all involved: the student, the instructor, supervisee, and the supervisor. Further, as discussed in Chapter 1, because we live in an age of classroom conflicts, cancel culture, and polarized politics, professors, students, supervisors, and trainees may feel concerned—or even anxious and fearful—that any comment they make on a sexual topic may—whether or not misheard, misinterpreted, taken out of context, purposefully distorted, or secretly recorded and destined to become a viral hit—might serve as a weapon that can be used against them.

The Topic of Sexual Reactions Is More Complex Than the Topic of Sexual Involvement

The topic of sexual attractions, arousals, and fantasies about patients may be much more frustratingly complex, uncertain, variable, unpredictable, ambiguous, and elusive than that of therapist–patient sexual intercourse or other physical, sexual involvement. Exploring sexual feelings about patients may not be as likely to lead to a clear sense of closure, conclusion, or confidence about what will follow as examining the issue of therapist–patient sexual contact. One fundamental difference is this: A therapist's engaging in sexual activity with a patient is a voluntary behavior on the therapist's part. As a voluntary behavior, it is something that the therapist can control. By contrast, few would argue that attractions, physiological reactions, and fantasies are always or even generally susceptible to voluntary control. That the therapist may, at any time, be vulnerable to a flow of spontaneous, surprising, and "uncontrolled" feelings or thoughts may make the topic of such reactions much more challenging to address with certainty or confidence.

One reason for this difficulty likely has to do with the immediacy of our reactions. Research suggests that sexual feelings in psychotherapy are widespread, yet relatively few professionals engage in therapist–patient sex (Pope et al., 2021). The overwhelming majority of therapists can honestly assure themselves that they are not among those who have violated the prohibition against sexually exploiting patients. Most, however, have felt sexual attraction toward a patient. Thus, the topic of therapist–patient sexual contact may have less personal immediacy than the topic of sexual feelings. Sexual involvement with a patient tends to be an act a small subset of other therapists do; sexual feelings toward a patient tends to be something we ourselves experience.

Another fundamental difference that enhances the complexity of sexual reactions to patients (vs. sexual behavior) is that the profession has reached a consensus on sexual involvement with patients. That view is: "Don't do it. No matter what." There is a clear and explicit prohibition against the behavior. Engaging in sex with patients is wrong under any circumstances. It is unethical, and it places patients at risk for harm. On the other hand, there is no one concrete standardized set of guidelines by which therapists can understand the meaning and implication of feeling sexually attracted to a patient. Actually, there cannot be. Every therapist is unique, every patient is unique, and every situation is both different and constantly evolving. Understanding the meaning and implications of sexual feelings must take into account this ambiguity. Fortunately, some resources are designed to help therapists manage the complexity in clinically and ethically appropriate ways (e.g., APA, 2007; Shelton, 2020).

So far, we have discussed the context of the problem of the unspoken, the nature of the problem in our profession, and barriers to overcoming the problem and speaking up, and have provided a specific example of the problem. In the next four chapters, we focus on strengthening our readiness and skills to speak up about challenging and complex unspoken topics.

PART **II** PREPARING TO
BREAK THE SILENCE

5
LOOKING INWARD

A Self-Assessment of How We Respond to Challenging Topics

Becoming a skilled psychotherapist seems *relatively* easy when considered a spectator sport. We therapists could read the writings and listen to the lectures of expert therapists, researchers, and teachers. We could study other people—mainly our clients—and try to understand and help them.

It can become harder—and feel more threatening or discouraging—to look within ourselves and learn what we need to know about ourselves to become competent, skilled, self-aware therapists who practice what we preach. We're probably all aware of that blissfully unaware person

- who claims to be helping someone else but is acting in a passive-aggressive, controlling, or otherwise unhelpful (and obnoxious) way;

- who, behind someone's back, criticizes the person's behavior, traits, or personality, and all the while, we're thinking to ourselves, "Do you really have no clue that you are describing yourself?"; and/or

- who would be genuinely shocked, angry, and offended if you suggested (accurately) that something they'd just said or done was condescending, hurtful, insulting, cruel, antisemitic, sexist, or racist.

https://doi.org/10.1037/0000350-006
Speaking the Unspoken: Breaking the Silence, Myths, and Taboos That Hurt Therapists and Patients, by K. S. Pope, N. Y. Chavez-Dueñas, H. Y. Adames, J. L. Sonne, and B. A. Greene

Becoming genuinely self-aware and gaining self-knowledge takes courage, work, resilience, and persistence. The journey to self-awareness is complicated by our blind spots, biases, and other barriers. It also forces us to leave the comfort and familiarity of our protective self-image, how we like to see ourselves, or how we want others to see us. And, like the ability to respectfully listen when others speak about taboo topics or voice views in conflict with our values and beliefs, being self-aware and gaining self-knowledge require humility and openness. We must summon the courage and willingness to consider—*truly* consider—possibilities that make us confused, anxious, angry, or afraid.

This chapter invites us into the hard work of looking inward, exploring, reflecting on, and talking about our experiences with unspoken topics by responding to a series of questions. Confronting these questions lays the groundwork for the more extensive explorations with others we present later in the book. We start to recognize and break the silence within ourselves first; then we can move to speaking up with others. When breaking the silence about a topic that is deeply challenging, we can see that we are not the infallible experts bringing the tablets of truth down from the mountain so that the ignorant may accept our teachings. (Anyone smiling at that sentence? Does anyone have a teacher who might fit that description without too much trouble?)

We invite you and others to join us in exploring difficult topics. We are seeking mutual support on a challenging journey. The more we know about who *we* really are, including our strengths, weaknesses, and tendencies and about how our inner life affects our behavior, the better partners we'll be with others in exploring difficult topics.

THE LOOKING INWARD SELF-ASSESSMENT

Meaningful self-assessment depends on the hard work of staying focused and thoroughly responding to the questions openly, honestly, and directly while maintaining a mindful awareness of your thoughts and emotions. Figure 5.1 illustrates three strategies that may be helpful as you begin this process. The arrows in the figure represent the reflexive and recursive nature of the Looking Inward Self-Assessment, developed by Pope, Chavez-Dueñas, Adames, Sonne, and Greene. Engagement with one strategy informs subsequent strategies in an ongoing, repeated fashion. This model emphasizes that exploration, learning, and growth form the foundation of, but are also the result of, self-knowledge and self-awareness and that they are rarely a linear process. Because we are constantly changing in some way, we'll never know all there is to know about ourselves. The person we are today is not exactly the same person we were yesterday.

FIGURE 5.1. The Looking Inward Self-Assessment

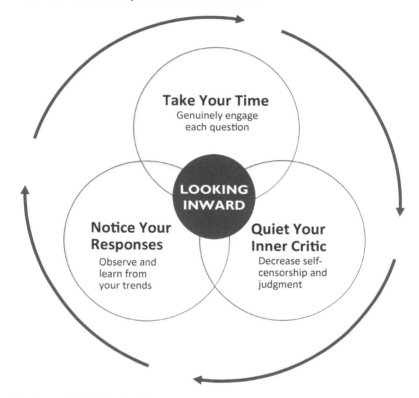

Note. Copyright 2023 by K. S. Pope, N. Y. Chavez-Dueñas, H. Y. Adames, J. L. Sonne, and B. A. Greene.

First Strategy

Take your time. Don't feel you need to read and respond to every single question in one sitting. Trying to plow through all of the questions without a break while doing justice to each area of inquiry would be challenging, if not impossible, and likely counterproductive. Instead, browse the focus areas in Table 5.1 and pick a few of the nine sections on which to focus at first. Set aside more than one session for this self-assessment and determine the length of each session by paying close attention to your stamina and ability to stay genuinely engaged with the questions presented in this chapter.

Second Strategy

Try to turn down the volume of your internal censor during your self-assessment sessions. Some of your responses may evoke a censoring reaction that you are

TABLE 5.1. The Looking Inward Self-Assessment Focus Areas

Section	Focus area
1	Potential Taboo-Enforcing Training Conditions in Your Graduate Program, Practicum, Internship, or Postdoctoral Training
2	General Clues to Tough Topics for You Personally
3	Your Clients' Feelings, Thoughts, Fantasies, or Behavior and Their Impact on You
4	Your Clients' Feelings, Thoughts, and Fantasies About You Specifically
5	Your Physical Self (Appearance and Behavior)
6	Your Clients' Physicality (Appearance and Behavior)
7	Physical Contact With a Client
8	Money and Fees
9	Speaking Up

ignorant, immature, confused, "politically incorrect" or "emotionally incorrect," biased, prejudiced, insulting, intolerant, or dangerous. You may convince yourself that you're entirely unsuited to be a therapist and should resign in shame from humanity. Instead, we hope you can be mindful of your judgmental voice. Learning about that critical voice and how it affects your learning is part of this exercise in strengthening self-awareness and self-knowledge. We hope you'll move on, perhaps noting the critical responses as clues to why you avoid certain topics.

Third Strategy

Take notes regarding your responses. You may notice trends regarding the relative difficulty of different topics raised in the questions that will be helpful in your later explorations with others. For example, with what topics or themes do you have most difficulty engaging? What makes those topics hard for you? What strategies can you create for dealing with those topics, particularly as you begin to speak up with others (later in the book)?

THE QUESTIONS

In this section, we present questions in nine focus areas (see Table 5.1). The areas and questions have been helpful to the authors of this book in our own development, in the classes and workshops we've led, and in our supervising and providing consultation to therapists and therapists-in-training.

Focus Area 1: Potential Taboo-Enforcing Training Conditions in Your Graduate Program, Practicum, Internship, or Postdoctoral Training

- Were there any taboo topics that went either unmentioned or were talked about in the most superficial, stilted, or abstract terms? If so, what were they?

- Did you ever do anything with a client you were reluctant to mention to your supervisor?
  - Did you ever tell your supervisor?
  - If so, did you tell your supervisor the whole story, including the parts that made you reluctant?
  - What were your reasons for making this choice?

- Did you ever later regret bringing up a topic, disclosing something, or taking a stance? If so, what was it, and why did you regret it?

- What factors—including different kinds of individual dynamics, social or cultural factors, interpersonal dynamics, group process, and organizational structure—seemed to foster secrets, taboos, and avoidance of important topics? For you personally, what factors seem to facilitate secrets, taboos, and avoidance of important topics?

- In what ways, if any, could openness, directness, and honesty be a liability?

- Did anyone ever pay the price for questioning an assumption, an approach, a rule, a professor, a supervisor, or anyone or anything else? If so, what was the price?

- Were any patients ever disparaged, ridiculed, or spoken about disrespectfully when they were not present?
  - If so, how would you characterize the patients who were the targets of these comments?
  - Did they share any common characteristics?

- Were the concerns of any patients ever ignored, minimized, or invalidated? If so, how would you describe the patients whose concerns were characterized this way?

- Were any students ever disparaged, ridiculed, or spoken about in a disrespectful manner?
  - Were they present?
  - Did these targets share any common characteristics?

- Were any students often ignored, passed over for opportunities, or silenced in class?
  - Were concerns they brought up minimized or ignored?
  - Or were they described as troublemakers or agitators?
  - Were the students who were treated like this similar in any kind of way?
- Were any faculty or supervisors ever disparaged, ridiculed, or spoken about, or spoken to disrespectfully?
  - Were they present?
  - Did these targets share any common characteristics?
- Was there any competitiveness (stop laughing!)? In what ways, if any, did the competitiveness play a role in shaping what could and could not be said, acknowledged, or questioned?
- Did you or any of your peers ever discuss feelings of incompetence, of being in over your head, of feeling overwhelmed or confused?
  - In what context?
  - How were such discussions received or handled, and by whom?
- Were there any barriers to access for people with disabilities?
  - Were these barriers addressed?
  - If so, how?
- Did you discuss race and ethnicity?
  - Were the discussions, in your opinion, honest, helpful, and adequate?
  - Were any aspects of race and ethnicity off-limits?
  - Were racism and White supremacy culture part of the conversation?
- How were issues of sex, gender, and sexual and affectional orientation discussed?
  - Were the discussions, in your opinion, honest, helpful, and adequate?
  - Were any aspects of sex, gender, and sexual and affectional orientation off-limits?
- What discussions involved issues of money (e.g., fees, your socioeconomic status [SES], your client's SES)?
  - Were the discussions, in your opinion, honest, helpful, and adequate?
  - Were any aspects of the topic of money off-limits?

- Were some supervisors easier to talk to about difficult topics than others? What characteristics in those supervisors contributed to that ease?

Focus Area 2: General Clues to Tough Topics for You Personally

- If there are certain kinds of clients who make you uncomfortable, how would you describe them?

- How, if at all, does your discomfort affect your ability to work effectively with them?

- To what extent do you acknowledge or discuss your discomfort with your supervisor?

- To what extent do you feel the need to consult with a colleague about your discomfort with them?

- To what extent is your discomfort acknowledged or reflected in your notes?

- Was there ever anything that happened in a therapy session with a client that you found yourself troubled or anxious about for a time after the session? What happened?

- During a session with a client, have you ever had feelings you were ashamed of?
  - What evoked those feelings?
  - How did you respond to your feelings?

- If your clients could, beginning right now, read your mind—including, but not limited to, all the thoughts and feelings you've had about them—what thought or feeling would be most surprising to them?

- If your clinical supervisors in graduate school, practica, internship, or postdoc could, beginning right now, read your mind—including, but not limited to, all the thoughts and feelings you've had about them—what thought or feeling would be most surprising to them?

Focus Area 3: Your Clients' Feelings, Thoughts, Fantasies, or Behavior and Their Impact on You

- Do you ever cry or tear up during therapy sessions?
  - If so, what moved you to tears?
  - How did the client respond?

- Does this seem to happen more with clients who identify as men or with clients who identify as women?
- What about transgender clients?
- Or does it equally happen with clients regardless of their gender?

• With what client(s) have you felt most intimate? How did you express the intimacy?

• Have you ever experienced the following feelings when you were with a therapy or counseling client?

- embarrassment
- jealousy
- upset
- anger
- fear
- disgust
- hatred

Now that you have reflected on whether you have experienced certain feelings toward clients in therapy, you can answer the following questions about each of the feelings you endorsed when responding to the preceding Focus Area 3 questions:

• What, if anything, could a client say or do to you that would make you feel _____ during the session?

• What contributed to feeling _____ toward your therapy client?

• Could you work effectively with a client with whom you felt _____?

• Have you ever made a mistake with a client because you felt _____?

• What, if anything, could a client say or do to you that you'd be embarrassed to tell your supervisor about?

• What, if anything, could a client say or do to you that you'd be embarrassed putting in the client's chart?

• Under what circumstances would you let the client know that you felt _____?

• Under what circumstances would you disclose that you felt _____ about your client to your supervisor?

• Under what circumstances would you mention in your notes that you felt _____ toward your client?

- Have you ever been so upset over something that has happened in therapy or so concerned about a patient that it interfered with your sex life?
- Have you ever fantasized about a client while you masturbated or had sex with someone else (who was not your client)?
  - Did you reflect on the fantasy later?
  - Did your awareness of the fantasy affect the therapy or your relationship with the client?
  - Did you have any positive reactions to your fantasy (e.g., excitement, pride, curiosity)?
  - Did you have any negative reactions to your fantasy (e.g., anxiety, guilt, fear, uncomfortable confusion)?
- Under what circumstances would you let the client know that you were sexually aroused by them?
- Under what circumstances would you disclose your sexual arousal to your supervisor?
- Under what circumstances would you mention your sexual arousal in your notes?
- Have you ever had a sexual fantasy or daydream during a therapy session?
  - If yes, did it involve the client?
  - Did it seem to have any meaning for the therapy or your relationship with the client?
- Does a client's sexual orientation evoke any particular feelings in you?
- Do you generally find yourself more sexually attracted to people of a certain race or ethnicity? If so, what implications might this have for how you conduct therapy?
- Has a client ever talked about their sexual experiences or fantasies in a way that you found enjoyable?
  - If yes, do you think that the client was aware of your enjoyment?
  - If so, how do you think this awareness might have affected or influenced the client?
- Have you ever reacted to a client's sexual talk or behavior with anger?
- Have you ever reacted to a client's sexual talk or behavior with fear?
- Have you ever reacted to a client's sexual talk or behavior with anxiety?

- Have you ever reacted to a client's sexual talk or behavior with guilt?

- Have you ever reacted to a client's sexual talk or behavior with embarrassment?

- Have you ever reacted to a client's sexual talk or behavior with intense curiosity?

- Does your sexual orientation affect your responses to clients' discussions of sexual feelings or behaviors? If so, how?

- Do you believe that it is possible that you may have acted seductively, fearfully, angrily, or hatefully toward a client without your being aware of it?

Focus Area 4: Your Clients' Feelings, Thoughts, and Fantasies About You Specifically

- Has a client ever told you something about your appearance that you found hurtful?
  - If yes, what was it?
  - How did you respond?

- Has a client ever told you something about your appearance that you found anxiety arousing?
  - If yes, what was it?
  - How did you respond?

- Has a client ever told you something about your appearance that you found pleasing?
  - If yes, what was it?
  - How did you respond?

- Do you believe that a client has ever imagined what your body would look like if you were not wearing any clothes? If yes, what feelings does this evoke in you?

- Has a client ever told you that they were upset with you? If yes, what feelings did that evoke in you?

- Does your client's gender affect how you respond to a client's discussion of feeling upset with you?

- Does your client's sexual and affectional orientation affect how you respond to a client's discussion of feeling upset with you?

- Does your client's ethnicity or race affect how you respond to a client's discussion of feeling upset with you?

Focus Area 5: Your Physical Self (Appearance and Behavior)

- Can you remember a time during a therapy session when you became privately aware of your appearance?
  - If yes, what did you become aware of?
  - What seemed to trigger this awareness?
- Can you remember a time during a therapy session when your appearance concerns (e.g., food stuck in your teeth, a hole in your clothing) became apparent to you and your client? If yes, how did you respond?
- Can you remember a time when you became privately but intensely aware of your own body during a therapy session?
  - If yes, what did you become aware of?
  - What seemed to lead to this awareness?
- Can you remember a time when your bodily processes (e.g., a burp, a stomach rumble) became obvious not only to you but also to your client? If so, how did you respond?
- During a therapy session, have you ever had the impulse to get up and move about (e.g., to stretch, to relieve the tension in your arms and legs, to help you "wake up")? If so, how did you respond to this impulse?
- Have you ever fallen asleep during a therapy session or felt very close to falling asleep? If so, how did you respond?
- Under what conditions would you partially disrobe during a session?
- Under what conditions would you completely disrobe during a session?

Focus Area 6: Your Clients' Physicality (Appearance and Behavior)

- Has a client ever dressed in a way that made you uncomfortable?
  - If yes, what was the nature of your discomfort?
  - How did you respond to feelings of discomfort?
- Is there anything about a client's physicality, characteristics, or disabilities that make you uncomfortable in any way?

- Does your sexual and affectional orientation affect your responses to clients' physical attributes?
- What is the most private part of a client's body you have seen?
  - How did your viewing this part of their body come about?
  - Was it apparent to the client that a private part of their anatomy was exposed?
  - Was it apparent to the client that you noticed?
  - Did either you or the client mention the incident?
  - What feelings did it seem to evoke in the client?
  - What feelings did it evoke in you?
- Has a client ever touched their genitals in your presence? If so, what feelings did this evoke in you?
- Have you ever become aware of a client's body odor?
  - If yes, what feelings did this evoke in you?
  - How did you respond to those feelings?
- Have you ever imagined what a client's body would look like if they were not wearing any clothes?
  - If yes, what feelings did this imaginary scene evoke in you?
  - Do you think the client was ever aware that you were creating this imaginary scene?
  - If they had been aware, what feelings do you think it might have evoked in them?
- Under what conditions would you allow a client to disrobe partially during a session?
- Under what conditions would you allow a client to disrobe entirely during a session?
- Has a client ever seemed to become sexually aroused or excited in your presence?
  - If yes, what seemed to cue you to your client's arousal?
  - What feelings did that evoke in you?
  - How, if at all, was the arousal discussed?
- Under what conditions would you show a client how to use a condom?

- Under what conditions would you show a client how to insert a tampon?

- Under what conditions would you examine a female client's chest and nipples?

- Under what conditions would you examine a male client's chest and nipples?

- Under what conditions would you examine a transgender client's chest and nipples?

Focus Area 7: Physical Contact With a Client

- Under what circumstances would you hold a client's hand?
  - Have you ever held a client's hand?
  - If yes, how did you feel?
  - How, if at all, did the client's age, gender, sexual and affectional orientation, race, culture, religion, or other factors affect the situation?

- Under what circumstances would you put your arm around a client?
  - Have you ever put your arm around a client?
  - If yes, how did you feel?
  - How, if at all, did the client's age, gender, sexual and affectional orientation, race, culture, religion, or other factors affect the situation?

- Under what circumstances would you hug a client? How, if at all, would the client's age, gender, sexual and affectional orientation, race, culture, religion, or other factors affect your decision?

- Have you ever hugged a client or been hugged by a client in such a way that seemed to have sexual overtones for you or for the client?
  - If yes, what did you feel?
  - What did you do?

- Has a client ever initiated a hug or kiss that you did not want?
  - If yes, what feelings did it evoke?
  - How did you handle the situation?

- Under what circumstances would you kiss a client on the cheek or forehead? How, if at all, would the client's age, gender, sexual and affectional orientation, race, culture, religion, or other factors affect your decision?

- Have you ever kissed a client on the cheek or forehead? If yes, how did you feel?

- Do you touch your male clients more, female clients more, transgender clients more, or all people equally?

- Under what circumstances would you have dinner with a client? How, if at all, would the client's age, gender, sexual and affectional orientation, race, culture, religion, or other factors affect your decision?

- Have you ever had dinner with a client? If yes, how did you feel?

- Under what circumstances would you go to a client's home? How, if at all, would the client's age, gender, sexual and affectional orientation, race, culture, religion, or other factors affect your decision?

- Have you ever gone to a client's home? If yes, how did you feel?

- Under what circumstances would you enter a client's bedroom? How, if at all, would the client's age, gender, sexual and affectional orientation, race, culture, religion, or other factors affect your decision?

- Have you ever entered a client's bedroom? If yes, how did you feel?

- Suppose you could be given an absolute assurance that you would suffer no negative consequences (e.g., no one else would ever know and there would be no complaint to a licensing board, ethics committee, civil court, or criminal court). Would you ever be tempted to enter into a sexual relationship with one of your clients?
  - What factors would you take into account in your considerations?
  - What would you decide?

Focus Area 8: Money and Fees

- Has it ever been hard to talk with a client about fees?

- Has it ever been hard to talk about a client's overdue bill for services?

- Have you ever reduced or waived your fee for a client?
  - If so, why?
  - Did you offer that same fee reduction to other clients in similar financial situations?

- Have you ever felt angry with a client regarding fees for service?
  - If so, what happened?
  - How did you respond to your anger?

- Have you ever felt guilt, shame, or otherwise uncomfortable with a client from a distinctly different socioeconomic background from you (either much lower or much higher SES)?

Focus Area 9: Speaking Up

- What topics would you be reluctant to speak up about in the following environments?
  - in class
  - in supervision
  - in consultation
  - with a client
  - with your own therapist
  - at a professional conference
- What topics do you feel trigger you because of your personal history?
- Have you ever found yourself keeping silent when you wished you could speak up?
  - If yes, what were the circumstances?
  - What were the costs and benefits of staying quiet?
  - How would you describe the short- and long-term effects of remaining silent?

How hard was staying focused and responding to the questions openly, honestly, and completely? Were you able to maintain a mindful awareness of your thoughts and feelings? If not, were there any similarities in the types of questions that raised your inner critic's voice or sent your attention off track from the task? Which questions were most important and personally meaningful to you?

Knowing *how* we personally respond to various challenging topics will deepen and enrich our self-knowledge. It will also help us navigate our attempts to discuss difficult topics with others, the focus of the next chapter.

6 STRENGTHENING THE COURAGE TO SPEAK UP

Creating a Supportive Context

Creating a culture of speaking up benefits us all. Our work as therapists grows stronger as we recognize, explore, and confront the silence, myths, and taboo topics that plague our profession and block or distort how we understand our clients. In the previous chapter, we conducted a personal self-assessment to increase our own awareness of our emotional and cognitive reactions to various unspoken or difficult topics. In this chapter, we move to the challenge of actually starting to speak with others about them when doing so may feel unsafe, uncomfortable, and risky.

To prepare for that challenge, we describe how to create a learning context that supports the courage necessary to begin acknowledging and discussing difficult topics in open and honest ways. This will provide a foundation for engaging with the topics that are the focus of Chapters 7 through 15 (see Chapter 2 for the list of topics).

https://doi.org/10.1037/0000350-007

Speaking the Unspoken: Breaking the Silence, Myths, and Taboos That Hurt Therapists and Patients, by K. S. Pope, N. Y. Chavez-Dueñas, H. Y. Adames, J. L. Sonne, and B. A. Greene

CREATING COURAGEOUS CONTEXTS

We all vary in our perspectives and perceptions of the learning contexts that support our courage to practice speaking up. Some of us feel braver in a small group of people we know well, like in a study or practice group. Others prefer larger groups of strangers, such as weekend workshops for therapists from a broad geographical area. Members of your learning group may all be known to you or share similar experiences with you (e.g., being new or experienced therapists, beginning graduate school together, working in independent practice, being members of a peer supervision group working from similar theoretical orientations). Or they may be known to you but have different experiences and interests (e.g., career stages, theoretical orientations, cultures, life experiences). Also, you may intentionally or unintentionally form or enter a group with several relative strangers (e.g., therapists from diverse geographical areas who have come together for a continuing education workshop). You may even decide to first complete all the exercises with a group of people similar to you and then reengage in the activities with a group of people quite different from you. Regardless of your preference, we encourage you to partner with at least one other person as you work on the exercises in Chapters 7 through 15.

Once you've selected those you'll be working with on the exercises, you'll need to make a few decisions together. Here's a list to help you get started:

- Will your group have a designated leader, share or rotate leadership, or work as a leaderless group?

- Would it be helpful to have other designated roles, such as timekeeper, group process observer, scenario/question reader, or checker for maintenance of safety conditions?

- When and how often do you want to meet, how long will the meetings be, and do you want to focus on one topic per session or have some other arrangement?

We suggest that the first meeting allow time to create and deepen a supportive context. In your first meeting, each member engaging in the exercises may be asked to identify the interpersonal conditions that best promote their courage and, if necessary, they may work on creating those conditions. This process requires special attention to members of minoritized communities.

For example, suppose the group comprises individuals across the gender and racial spectrum. In these instances, creating a courageous context may require an open discussion of how it is healthy to distrust systems, institutions, and people that have contributed to oppression. Such discussion signals that, in this place or with this person, we can talk about the history and inhumanity experienced by those historically and currently oppressed. It is also important to pay attention to other factors that may undermine someone's feelings of trust and of being heard and respected by the group. For example, someone with politically or socially conservative beliefs may fear their contributions will be unwelcome or discounted if everyone else in the group is liberal. Or a person with a physical disability may dread being treated—once again— as the spokesperson for everyone who has a disability when the group begins the exercises in Chapter 7.

In the authors' experience, it is helpful to discuss five actions for supporting participants' courage and to commit to each person's active involvement in self-examination and communication with others:

- Understand, appreciate, and value your role as an active participant.

- Remain curious and open to your self-discoveries and what others disclose.

- Cultivate humility and safeguard mutual respect for all participants.

- Create a balance between respecting the privacy of others while resisting colluding with the human tendency to pull back into silence during challenging conversations by inviting each other to speak up.

- From time to time, check to see if anyone is feeling anxious, uncomfortable, threatened, disrespected, misunderstood, discounted, or silenced.

What reactions are you having to the five conditions? What does each person think and feel about the conditions? Are there other conditions that are necessary for people to feel courageous? In the next sections, we expand on each of the five conditions.

Condition 1: Understand, Appreciate, and Value Your Role as an Active Participant

Our approach to speaking up is based on introspection, self-reflection, self-questioning, self-monitoring of our thoughts and feelings, *and* interpersonal risk-taking. It differs from many workshops, courses, and books for which participants assume a more passive-receptive role, absorbing that what the instructor, leader, supervisor, or book teaches is "the way" to define and think about topics.

This volume does not provide a set of "right answers" and doesn't take a cookbook approach to enormously complex, often controversial issues. Instead, the goal is to increase our self-awareness, our understanding of factors and processes that influence how—and sometimes whether—we approach difficult topics, and our ability to overcome silencing so we can speak up. We also believe that it is vital for therapists to develop skills to effectively address issues that are often ambiguous and controversial, without easy, clear, or straightforward answers.

Condition 2: Commit to Curiosity and Openness

Fundamental to speaking up is our ability to be curious and open to discovering, sharing, and examining our reactions to the passages and scenarios in Chapters 7 through 15 of this volume and to hear and reply respectfully, openly, and supportively to the responses of others. This is true whether we're just starting our training or have years or decades of clinical experience. Curiosity and openness within the context of speaking up serve crucial functions, including identifying our own internal rules and assumptions, helping us see new possibilities and change our behaviors, and prompting others to explore, discover, consider, and learn.

Condition 3: Maintain Humility and Safeguard Mutual Respect

Maintaining humility and safeguarding respect for our colleagues and their contributions to the learning process can be challenging in this situation because one goal is to put words to the all-too-often unspeakable. People reveal a lot about themselves when they begin to explore uncharted territory, even when discussing hypothetical cases. Differences among participants in feelings, attitudes, values, thoughts, and experiences may be perceived by others as defects, deviance, immaturity, ignorance, prejudice, psychopathology, or traits inconsistent with being a good therapist. Cultivating humility, appreciating and respecting differences, and maintaining awareness that we all have a lot to learn and contribute can help us set aside any tendencies to label, demean, dismiss, shame, interrupt, and shut down those whose reactions are different— a critical step in speaking the unspoken.

Condition 4: Find a Balance

This learning experience aims to speak about the "unspeakable"—to bring topics that have been very private, difficult, or off limits into the open. The advantage of navigating this process with others is that one participant's biases, fears, or resistances may be recognized, validated, and gently challenged by fellow group members. However, others' pushing or pressuring can jeopardize another member's willingness to exercise courage. Because participants will vary in their need for privacy, often according to the taboo topic on the table, it will likely be helpful for each participant to clarify how they will communicate their need for space to the group.

Conversely, the group may experience a "pull" to maintain silence on a topic. Rather than pushing too hard, members begin to sabotage the exploration process. For instance, participants may unintentionally or deliberately disrupt the learning process with interruptions, distractions, attacks, trite statements, withdrawal into apparent boredom or drowsiness, or other misdirecting or blocking maneuvers. Of course, the pullback toward silencing the unspoken is expected. Periodically asking members to mention any signs of sabotage and to consider what is *not* being discussed may be helpful.

Condition 5: Check for Threats to the Courageous Context

In addition to an initial discussion of each of the conditions needed for exercising courage, it is critically important that group members check in regularly for any threats to those conditions. Ideally, participants will feel comfortable raising concerns when any potential or experienced threat occurs. However, participants who are not feeling courageous may simply withdraw and become silent instead of discussing their concerns. Regular safety check-ins can help identify this process. As mentioned earlier, the group may decide the frequency of safety checks and who will be responsible for leading them in their initial meeting. Group members may also discuss how to adjust or change conditions that may fuel any threats within the group. Table 6.1 provides a checklist of

TABLE 6.1. Checklist of Effective Conditions for Learning and Strengthening Abilities to Speak Up

Session	Tasks
First group meeting	_____ Each member discusses the interpersonal conditions that facilitate and promote their courage to speak up.
	_____ Each member commits to *active* involvement in group explorations.
	_____ Each member agrees to maintain humility and safeguard mutual respect.
	_____ Each member describes how they will communicate a need for space.
	_____ Each member suggests how to address potential sabotage of the discussion.
	_____ A group member agrees to take responsibility for monitoring the initial session checklist and initiating check-ins.
	_____ The group decides on the frequency of check-ins.
Subsequent check-ins	_____ Is each member's sense of a courageous context in the learning group being supported?
	_____ Is each group member actively involved?
	_____ Are all members showing humility and mutual respect?
	_____ Is the group honoring members' requests for space?
	_____ Is the group honoring a commitment to address sabotage?

the five conditions we have outlined and is designed for easy reference as we move toward the exercises in Chapters 7 through 15 that challenge us to speak the unspoken.

Now that we have discussed creating conditions that support becoming courageous and speaking up, let's move on to introduce the learning exercises.

INTRODUCING THE LEARNING EXERCISES

As described earlier, authentic communication is essential to meaningful and effective work with our clients, supervisees, consultees, and professional colleagues. Such discussion requires us to think clearly, talk openly, and listen respectfully. To do that, we must overcome the all-too-common implicit and explicit rules and myths that interfere with the genuine and honest examination, questioning, deliberation, and discussion. Certain sensitive topics trigger our tendencies to fall back on those rules and myths and work to impose silence. We are likely then to discount, preempt, dismiss, ignore, stereotype, shame, scorn, and attack those we disagree with. We limit our readings and discussions to those that reflect and reinforce our views. We rely on unsupported assumptions, outdated theories, and conventional practices.

The nine chapters that follow provide exercises designed to help mental health professionals begin to acknowledge, understand, and challenge our silencing tendencies and to begin speaking up. Each set of activities focuses on one of the nine challenging topics (see the list in Chapter 2) that have been historically hard for our profession.

We anticipate that as you engage in these learning exercises, your self-awareness and comfort with speaking up about difficult topics will grow. We hope the activities will help prepare you to speak more openly, honestly, and directly with those you work with and serve.

PART **III** SPEAKING THE
UNSPOKEN—
EXERCISES FOR
EXPLORING AND
LEARNING

7 TALKING ABOUT PHYSICAL DIFFERENCE AND DISABILITY

We notice others' bodies, including those of our clients, if we have sight. We see physical differences (e.g., lower or higher than average weight, disfigurement, amputations, skin discoloration) and disabilities (e.g., disabilities caused by paralysis or traumatic brain injury).[1]

And, as social beings, most of us therapists have learned through life experience and socialization to extend the "tactful courtesy" of ignoring—or, probably more often, pretending to ignore—what seems to be different or unique about someone's body features or functions (Karson, 2018, p. 84). Alternately, we may find ourselves reflexively applying false stereotypes, scripts, or narratives about clients based solely on our perception, perspective, and interpretation of a physical or ability difference (Olkin, 1999).

---

[1]We recognize the continuing evolution of disability language over the past few years and underscore the importance of using the term "disability" and having flexibility in the use of person-first and identity-first disability language. We refer the reader to a recent article by Andrews et al. (2022) and the American Psychological Association (APA, 2021) inclusive language guidelines for further discussion of this topic.

https://doi.org/10.1037/0000350-008
Speaking the Unspoken: Breaking the Silence, Myths, and Taboos That Hurt Therapists and Patients, by K. S. Pope, N. Y. Chavez-Dueñas, H. Y. Adames, J. L. Sonne, and B. A. Greene

EXAMPLES OF FALSE STEREOTYPES, SCRIPTS, AND NARRATIVES

Here are some illustrations of false stereotypes:

- The person must be extremely courageous, strong, and determined for facing and overcoming daunting challenges every day.

- People with physical differences or disabilities are sources of inspiration.

- The person must be pitied for their presumed plight.

- Symptoms of depression or anxiety most likely result from the client's physical difference or disability.

- Some of the greatest barriers people with physical differences and disabilities face are environmental ones (e.g., furniture size and shape, door access, room size).

- The treatment plan needs to focus on the physical difference or disability.

- The goal of treatment must be to help the client adjust to their physical difference or disability.

- The best approach is to act like I don't notice any differences and not mention them unless the client speaks of them first.

- The best approach is to refer this person to a therapist who specializes in working with people who have this difference or disability.

Our scripts and narratives make it hard to see people with physical differences or disabilities as individuals rather than stereotypes—to see the actual person instead of the stereotype. The stereotypes, in turn, throw the psychotherapy process off course. They perpetuate therapists' own biases, false assumptions, and negative emotional and cognitive reactions to differences. They communicate the taboo nature of these topics to clients. They block open and authentic communication between the therapist and client. And they cut off any genuine understanding of our clients' actual experiences (Olkin, 1999).

Historically, our training as mental health professionals has contributed to the invisibility of people with physical differences and disabilities. Although we recognize differences and disabilities as essential elements of human diversity today, we fall short in providing courses and training opportunities that educate student therapists about the physical, emotional, sociocultural, and political issues involved (APA, 2022b; see also Andrews et al., 2019; Dunn & Andrews, 2015). Therapists-in-training are often left with little or no experience to counter their own narratives; they are ill equipped to provide clinically and ethically sound services to clients with differences and disabilities (APA, 2012a). As Olkin (1999) pointed out, this omission in our profession "reinforces the marginalization" of this client community (p. 305).

QUESTIONS FOR REFLECTION AND DISCUSSION

The exercise that follows offers the opportunity to explore some of these issues. We encourage you to be as open as possible in examining your internal processes and external influences.

Scenario: Imagine that you are meeting with a new client for an intake session. You see the client for the first time in the waiting room and observe that they weigh more than 300 pounds.

- What are your immediate emotional reactions?
  - Are you aware of any assumptions you may have regarding the reason for the client's large size or why the client is seeking therapy?
  - Do you have any thoughts about the therapy goals or how treatment will unfold?
  - Are you suddenly much more aware of your own weight and body size? Of the size and stability of the chair in your consulting room?
- Can you identify any times when anyone in your family talked to you about weight—yours or someone else's?
  - If yes, what did they say?
  - Can you identify any family "rules"—explicit or unspoken—about eating and weight in your family?
  - What has stayed with you?
- Have you ever considered the degree to which your beliefs about others' physical and cognitive functioning reflect *ableism*, an intentional or unintentional belief that there is a correct way for bodies and minds to function and that those who deviate from that way are inferior and need "fixing"? If so, are you more inclined toward those beliefs with certain kinds of physical differences and disabilities than with others?
- Have you thought about how you might approach providing therapy with clients who have physical differences or disabilities?
  - Is your office space (including the waiting room, therapy room, restrooms) physically accessible and comfortable (see Adames et al., 2023, pp. 37–38)?

- Have you considered the client's communication access needs (e.g., a quiet environment; specific technologies, such as sign language computers, documents in large print or Braille)?

• Have you thought about the language you typically use regarding clients with disabilities?

- Is it person-first language (e.g., "a woman with paralysis of both legs") or disability-first language (e.g., "a paraplegic woman")?
- Does it matter because there is no consensus among people with disabilities about person-first versus identity-first language (see Andrews et al., 2019, 2022; Dunn & Andrews, 2015)?
- How do cultural values influence which language we default to using?
- Does your language change when talking to someone with a physical difference versus an ability difference?
- Do you know which type of language the client prefers?
- Would you assume that the client is seeking therapy because of their disability?

• Do you have a physical difference or disability, whether visible or not?

- If yes, how do you think that affects your interactions with clients who have a similar or other difference or disability?
- How do you think it affects your interactions with clients who do not?

• When you think about your classroom discussions in this area and your formal and informal talks with teachers and students, what, if anything, seemed off limits or so sensitive that people grew uncomfortable when it was mentioned—or the discussion stayed superficial, "politically correct," or otherwise inauthentic?

Considering these questions is a step toward examining how our personal history and professional training have impacted our perspective on physical differences and disabilities. In turn, this awareness will help us be more mindful of how these views affect our work with clients who are members of this community.

8 TALKING ABOUT SEXUAL AND AFFECTIONAL ORIENTATION

Most of us find it hard to talk with complete openness and honesty about sexuality. We may grow nervous thinking about, much less discussing, our intimate feelings, thoughts, attractions, and behaviors with others. Giving voice to the topic of sexuality may bring up feelings of vulnerability or make us feel like we're breaking a social norm, engaging in a forbidden act, or doing something wrong. The beliefs about sexuality that our families, religions, cultural traditions, mass media, and society have instilled in us influence

- the degree to which we feel comfortable thinking and talking with others about sexuality;
- those we choose to talk to about sexuality;
- how we understand and make sense of sexuality; and
- the language we use to talk about sexuality, whether we speak directly or indirectly or openly or defensively and what terms we use.

Concerns about our safety or history of sexual abuse and harassment can also strengthen the collective silence around the topic. But sexuality is a normal part of human development, and talking about this difficult topic has its benefits (Fennell & Grant, 2019; S. M. Harris & Hays, 2008; Lung et al., 2021;

https://doi.org/10.1037/0000350-009
Speaking the Unspoken: Breaking the Silence, Myths, and Taboos That Hurt Therapists and Patients, by K. S. Pope, N. Y. Chavez-Dueñas, H. Y. Adames, J. L. Sonne, and B. A. Greene

Newman & Newman, 2017). For instance, talking about sexuality can counter the negative stigma affecting how we view ourselves, our bodies, and our sexual choices. It also helps increase self-awareness of sexual biases, values, and beliefs while normalizing talking about sexuality with others.

EXPANDING HOW WE TALK ABOUT SEXUALITY

Sexuality often centers on sexual orientation and sexual attraction. For instance, *sexual orientation* is typically described as "the sex of those to whom one is sexually and romantically attracted" (American Psychological Association, 2012b, p. 11; Fennell & Grant, 2019). This notion of sexual orientation tends to divide people into social categories like these, for instance:

- Gay and lesbian individuals are attracted to members of the same sex.
- Heterosexual people are attracted to people of another sex from their own.
- Bisexual people are attracted to both sexes.
- Asexual people experience little to no sexual attraction.
- Demisexual people only feel sexually attracted to someone when they have an emotional bond with the person.

However, this framework is restrictive. It fails to capture the nuanced experiences of actual individuals. For instance, its emphasis on "sex" does not consider the person's emotional or affectional attraction[1] based on gender (Adames & Chavez-Dueñas, 2021; Shively & De Cecco, 1977). These subtle but essential nuances contribute to how we talk about sexual orientation and can prevent us from discussing the topic openly and with confidence and curiosity.

The following questions can help us get started in examining how we talk about sexual and affectional orientation:

- What comes to mind when we hear "same-sex relationships" versus "same-gender-loving relationships"?

- How might a discussion centered on sex differ from one centered around gender?

- The American Psychological Association (2015) *Guidelines for Psychological Practice With Transgender and Gender Nonconforming People* embraced describing attraction in terms of gender (e.g., same-gender-loving relationships). Is there room for further expansion and curiosity?

---

[1]Affectional orientation expands our notion of sexual orientation. It underscores how people's attraction to others is not limited to sexuality but can also involve an emotional connection.

Adames and Chavez-Dueñas (2021) believed there is: They observed that, despite the expansion in our talks about sexual orientation, "these notions of sexual orientation continue to be myopic" (p. 62). They offered seven questions (p. 62) to help us stimulate discussion on the topic of sexual and affectional orientation:

- What exactly are we attracted to in others?
- Are we attracted to people's sex?
- Is it their gender?
- Gender expression?
- Is it the way that they talk, walk, dress, and communicate that romantically or emotionally draws us to others?
- Or can it be other aspects of the person's self that are appealing to us?
- Is attraction at first sight real?

How we respond to these questions about what we're attracted to in others provides a glimpse into how we were socialized regarding this topic. The following section focuses on how socialization shapes how we engage in or avoid discussing sexual and affectional orientation.

SOCIALIZATION SHAPES HOW WE THINK AND TALK ABOUT SEXUAL AND AFFECTIONAL ORIENTATION

Our work as therapists and clinical supervisors is shaped by our *personal socialization,* or the process through which we are taught the lessons, messages, and norms of our culture of origin. A key component of this process is our *gendered-sexual socialization,* which includes the messages we learn about the rules, beliefs, and expectations associated with gender roles, sexual behaviors, and sexuality (Adames & Chavez-Dueñas, 2021; Gansen, 2017).

Most of us are first exposed to, learn, and internalize messages in which the norms are heterosexuality and the permanence of the gender identity assigned at birth based on sex. These messages influence how we view ourselves and others as gendered and sexual beings and how we respond to and treat people who fall outside what society describes as the "norm." It is vital to recognize how our gendered-sexual socialization impacts each of us personally and professionally.

Looking inward, however, is not always easy, and when we do so in isolation, we are less likely to notice our prejudgments and assumptions. We may view ourselves as people who are open, accepting, and welcoming to all. Yet we may be unaware of some of our biases. Failing to examine and talk about our assumptions and prejudgments can negatively impact the therapeutic relationship.

QUESTIONS FOR REFLECTION AND DISCUSSION

In this exercise, we provide questions—each based on a scenario—for you to consider by yourself and with others.

Scenario 1

You have fond memories of a person you met in your early adult years, someone you had a serious crush on. Recently, they began following you on one of your social media apps. You go onto their profile, noticing that their gender pronouns have changed. They send you a DM [direct message] to say hello. They are interested in reconnecting and ask if you would like to catch up. Let's assume you're single or in an open relationship, and you learn that they are interested in a romantic relationship with you:

* What feeling and thoughts does their change evoke in you?
* How, if at all, does their change in pronouns affect your attraction to them?
* Would you respond and reconnect with them? Why or why not?

Scenario 2

You're having dinner with a friend whom you've known for some time. Recently, you've become closer, and they start sharing how upset they've been with people in their life who assume that their pansexuality is just a phase they are going through before coming out as gay or lesbian:

* What feelings do you experience?

* What questions come up for you as you're listening to your friend?

* What are your honest views of individuals who identify as pansexual?

* Do you feel comfortable asking your friend what pansexuality is, if you are not familiar with it?

    – What facilitates your asking?

    – If you are not asking, what's holding you back?

* If you're discussing this vignette in a class or other group setting, to what extent do you believe the discussion is limited by "political correctness"—fear

that honest responses will be viewed negatively by others? If it is limited by those or other factors, are there any steps the group might take to encourage and support more open and honest discussion?

Scenario 3

Your friend proceeds to share that pansexuality is not the same as bisexuality and that when others make this assumption, they feel invisible and silenced. They state, "How hard is it to understand that we pansexual people are not limited to biological sex, gender, or gender identity in our sexual and affectional attraction to others? We are limitless, unlike gay, lesbian, and bisexual people are."

- What are you feeling?
- Do you believe you understand what your friend is saying?
- Are you one of the people in your friend's life who has contributed to their feeling of invisibility?
- How would you respond to your friend?
- What are some thoughts and reactions you are having that you would not feel comfortable sharing with your friend?

Scenario 4

One of your clients is a 29-year-old cisgender man who identifies as asexual. He presents with symptoms of generalized anxiety disorder and panic attacks. Near the end of a recent session, your client reports that he will miss the next two sessions. He proceeds to share that he's getting married and will be away on his honeymoon. Your client says, "I did not share about my partner because it has never come up." You are surprised; you did not know the client was in a romantic relationship or engaged because he often described himself as asexual:

- What are your initial feelings and thoughts?
- What assumptions contributed to your not asking about the client's romantic relationship?
- What is your current understanding of asexuality, and what is it informed by?
- How would you respond to the client?
- How can you ensure that, in the future, you don't make assumptions about aspects of clients' sexuality?

Scenario 5

For more than a year, you have worked with a 30-year-old cisgender woman who self-identified as heterosexual. She sought treatment for symptoms related to anxiety that are affecting her ability to concentrate at work. Recently, the client expressed feeling "very confused" because she is experiencing attraction toward her coworker, a transgender man. In the last few sessions, she has begun to wonder why she is attracted to her coworker. She states, "I'm straight and attracted to men. Does this mean I am a lesbian?" Think about these questions:

• What are some things you need to consider in this situation?
• What emotional reactions does this scenario evoke in you?
• How would you respond to the client?
• Would your reactions change if the client were a cisgender man?
• How might the client's socialization contribute to her confusion?
• In what ways do you relate to the client?
• How has your training prepared or failed to prepare you to address the client's questions?
• How has your socialization impacted how you understand the situation?

We invite you to continue reflecting on your reactions to these scenarios and questions in this chapter. Resist moving away quickly from the vulnerability or unexpected or perhaps uncomfortable feelings that may surface when discussing sexual and affectional orientation.

9 TALKING ABOUT SEXUAL REACTIONS TO CLIENTS

It is an understatement to say that talking about sexual reactions to clients is challenging for many therapists. Chapter 4 traced the history of psychology's hesitancy and sometimes strong resistance to discussing this topic openly, honestly, and directly. We tend to find it hard to acknowledge that we sometimes feel sexually attracted to our clients, may even become sexually aroused in their presence, and fantasize about them (Pope et al., 1986; Pope, Keith-Spiegel, & Tabachnick, 2006). Conducting both a survey and focus groups, Vesentini et al. (2022) found that

> although therapists themselves highly recommend referring the client to a colleague if feelings become too intense, this rarely happens in practice. Most therapists consider talking about their romantic and sexual feelings towards clients as something very important, but only a third have disclosed their feelings in supervision, peer-supervision, or in personal therapy. Therapists indicate there is still hesitance about this due to fear of condemnation. (para. 1)

Considering this resistance, it's no surprise that graduate training has often stopped short of addressing these topics fully (Sonne & Jochai, 2014).

https://doi.org/10.1037/0000350-010
Speaking the Unspoken: Breaking the Silence, Myths, and Taboos That Hurt Therapists and Patients, by K. S. Pope, N. Y. Chavez-Dueñas, H. Y. Adames, J. L. Sonne, and B. A. Greene

The lack of adequate education in this area communicates to trainees and young professionals that it is not okay or appropriate to discuss sexual reactions to clients, which supports and continues the avoidance of the topic. We have few opportunities, then, to acknowledge, understand, and accept our own sexual feelings about our clients. Although some therapists and trainees may feel alone and ashamed when experiencing intense sexual feelings about a client, knowing the research in this area may be a reassuring first step in learning how to respond. For instance, research suggests that most therapists have felt sexually attracted to a client; that most reported experiencing guilt, anxiety, and confusion about the attraction; and that more than a fourth engaged in sexual fantasies about a client (for a review, see Pope et al., 2021).

QUESTIONS FOR REFLECTION AND DISCUSSION

The purpose of this exercise is to help therapists, supervisors, and trainees explore more fully and talk more openly about sexual attractions to clients. Before diving into the scenarios, consider these questions:

- Does it seem like the whole topic or specific aspects of the therapists' sexual reactions (attractions, arousal, fantasies) to their clients are off limits, taboo, or actively avoided in your clinical training and practice?

- Did you receive any messages that it was a good idea to stay away from openly acknowledging and talking about these reactions?

- What happened when someone tried to talk about these experiences? If no one tried, what do you imagine would happen if they did?

- Have you ever been aware of a sexual relationship between a graduate student and an educator (teacher, supervisor, administrator) in your training program?
  - If so, what did you think and feel about that?
  - Did you talk with anyone about it?
  - Do you think that your knowledge of that relationship affects your feelings about talking with a clinical supervisor about your sexual feelings regarding a client?

Scenario 1

Imagine you are a graduate student in clinical training. (This should be relatively easy for those who actually are graduate students in clinical training.) You suddenly find yourself sexually attracted to a client and feel aroused in their presence. That night, you have a vivid dream about them.

- Do you discuss all of this with your supervisor? Why or why not?
- What are some of your reactions as you imagine this scenario?
- Do you share your reactions with anyone else?

Scenario 2

Imagine a client who almost perfectly meets your private ideal of physical attractiveness. You even find it distracting at times. Suppose the client suddenly says, "I'm sensing you find me attractive. Is that accurate, or am I hallucinating? Do you?"

- What do you feel when the client expresses curiosity about your attraction toward them?
- What's the first reply that comes to mind? How do you think you'd actually reply?
- Do you discuss this with your supervisor, clinical consultant, or anybody else?

Scenario 3

While talking with a client, you accidentally refer to them using your partner's name.

- How do you feel?

- What thoughts occur to you?

- What, if anything, do you think you'd say to the client about your mistake?

- Would you discuss this with your supervisor, clinical consultant, or anyone else? Why or why not?

- Are there any aspects of your sexual feelings about clients that you'd be reluctant or unwilling to discuss with your supervisor or a clinical consultant, whether because of embarrassment, feeling unsafe, personal boundaries, or other reasons? If so, what are the reasons?

- How, if at all, do you think avoiding talking about these aspects affects training and practice?

Scenario 4

Suppose you decide to discuss your sexual feelings or attractions with your supervisor or clinical consultant.

- What language would you use to describe your experiences?

- As you imagine what you'd say, do you find yourself using words that are less that open, honest, and direct? Do they disguise or deflect your sexual feelings toward the client? Here's an example: "We have a very close therapeutic relationship" or "Our sessions have achieved a good level of trust and intimacy" versus "I am sexually aroused when I see my client" or "I find myself fantasizing about my client."

Scenario 5

Say you do talk with your supervisor or clinical consultant about your sexual attraction to a client.

- What do you feel as you leave the discussion?
- How likely are you to continue having such frank discussions about the same client or a different client with that supervisor or consultant?
- What factors might affect that likelihood?

Although speaking about sexual reactions to clients may not be easy, and we may not feel fully prepared or eager to do it, acknowledging that these feelings are common is critical. We hope the questions in this chapter helped you explore, reflect, and be more comfortable openly talking about this topic.

10 TALKING ABOUT ANGER

It is, of course, natural for therapists to get angry at their patients and for patients to get angry at their therapists. But it can sometimes be hard for us to acknowledge anger fully and address it effectively. The therapist's anger may seem a bad fit for the image of the therapist as a kind, caring, accepting healer. The patient's anger at the therapist may try the therapist's patience; clash with the therapist's wish to be appreciated; and, if sufficiently intense, frighten the therapist.

Part of the problem is that anger is often mistaken for aggression. However, there is a difference. *Anger* is a natural human emotion experienced in response to abuse, oppression, or perceived threat. In contrast, *aggression* is a behavior driven by the intent to cause harm to someone else. Because anger is confused with aggression, we often receive the message that anger is bad and should be suppressed rather than expressed. In our society, the expression of anger is particularly discouraged and weaponized against People of Color, women, people with disabilities, and other minoritized groups. In a National

https://doi.org/10.1037/0000350-011
Speaking the Unspoken: Breaking the Silence, Myths, and Taboos That Hurt Therapists and Patients, by K. S. Pope, N. Y. Chavez-Dueñas, H. Y. Adames, J. L. Sonne, and B. A. Greene

Public Radio podcast, Rutgers University professor Brittney Cooper captured how anger is used against Black women in particular:

> Whenever someone weaponizes anger against Black women, it is designed to silence them. It is designed to discredit them and to say that they don't have a good grasp on reality, that they are overreacting, that they are being hyper-sensitive, that whatever set of conditions that they are responding to, that their reaction is outsized. (Demby & Bates, 2019, para. 61; see also Cooper, 2018; Watson-Singleton, 2017)

Because of anger's bad rep, we learn how to hide and deny it in ourselves and tend to feel uncomfortable and threatened when others express anger or if we believe others might communicate it. We learn how to hide and deny anger in ourselves and try to control it in others. This pattern is also evident in psychology and other related health fields in which various programs have been developed for "anger management" rather than "aggression management."

As therapists, if we consider that anger is a normal response to abuse and oppression, attempting to control it in our clients hinders their ability to express their full humanity (Sommers-Flanagan, 2013). Instead of managing a client's anger, we can recognize it as a natural emotion and help them explore its meaning, understand its causes and implications, and find healthy ways to express it. That's easier said than done. Our own emotions and the messages we receive about anger from society and even our families get in the way. But anger can be transformative and constructive when nurtured (Sommers-Flanagan, 2013). In her influential essay on the uses of anger, Lorde (1997) stated,

> Focused with precision [anger] can become a powerful source of energy serving progress and change. And when I speak of change, I do not mean a simple switch of positions or a temporary lessening of tensions, nor the ability to smile or feel good. I am speaking of a basic and radical alteration in all those assumptions underlying our lives. . . . Anger expressed and translated into action in the service of our vision and our future is a liberating and strengthening act of clarification, for it is in the painful process of this translation that we identify who are our allies with whom we have grave differences, and who are our genuine enemies. Anger is loaded with information and energy. (p. 280)

QUESTIONS FOR REFLECTION AND DISCUSSION

The purpose of this exercise is to help us pause, reflect, and talk about the role of anger in our lives, society, and our work as therapists.

Scenario 1

You are taking a walk around the park when you notice a group of children playing on the playground. One of the kids is sitting on the ground, playing with a toy firetruck. A much older kid comes up to that younger child and says, "Give me your firetruck." The younger child responds, "No, it's mine." The older child proceeds to push the little one and takes the child's firetruck. The younger child grabs a handful of dirt and throws it at the older kid's face. Immediately, the older kid begins to cry profusely.

Suddenly, two women who appear to be the children's moms walk up to them. One of the women talks to the younger child and says, "Peter, why did you do that? That's not nice." Peter says, "I am mad at Billy. He pushed me and took my truck. That's not nice, either." Mom says, "Oh no, little Peter, being mad is not good. Go apologize to Billy and say you are sorry and that you are not mad at him."

In thinking about this scenario, reflect on your own experience with anger growing up in your family of origin and consider the following questions:

- What are some reactions you are having about how Peter's mom responded to what happened?

- What would you have done differently, if anything?

- Was anger an emotion that you were allowed to express growing up?
  - What messages did you receive about anger?
  - Were there limits on just what you could be angry about?

- Have you ever been afraid of anger—your own or someone else's? Why were you scared?

Scenario 2

Imagine yourself facilitating a group (e.g., therapy, supervision, consultation), and one of the participants tells another group member, "We can hear you—You'll need to lower your voice and not be so angry if you want people to hear what you have to say."

- What are your immediate emotional reactions as you read the scenario?

- What are some thoughts that come to mind as the interaction unfolds?

- What are some things you would need to consider in this case?

- Based on the demographics of the two group members, how would your reaction change?
  - For instance, what if the participant making the statement is a White man and the person being asked to "not be so angry" is a Woman of Color?
  - What if it were a Black man saying that to a White woman?

- From your perspective, what would be the ideal response to this scenario?

- How would your response differ, if at all, from how you are likely to respond in real life?

Scenario 3

You have been working with a client for approximately a year. Your work together has focused on the client's desire to "feel more authentic" in relationships. Sessions have focused on themes around "trusting self" and "uneasiness around expressing emotions." Over the past few weeks, the client has been, at times, expressing feelings of "being stuck" and unsure if therapy is working. At the end of the last session, the client sighs deeply and says, "Before I go today, I just want to say that I am freakin' pissed off. I don't think you're getting it."

- What are your immediate emotional reactions as you read the scenario?
- What are some thoughts that come to mind as you listen to your client and observe their frustration?
- What are some things you might consider in this situation?
- From your perspective, what would be a therapeutic response to this scenario?
- How would your response differ, if at all, from how you are likely to respond in real life?

Scenario 4

You have been working for a few months with a client who is a survivor of intergenerational violence. During your last session, the client says, "I know what happened to me is unfair, and it caused me so much pain, but I don't want to be angry." As you listen closely, the client proceeds and shares, "My mom always said anger is a poison that corrodes the soul. So, I keep thinking that the rage inside my heart needs to go away. I can't go on like this." The client continues, "Please show me how to drain all this poison so I can live in peace. How do I get rid of all this anger, doc?"

- What are your immediate emotional reactions as you read the scenario?

- How does your own socialization and the messages you learned about anger growing up impact your initial reaction to the client in this case?

- What thoughts come to mind as you listen to your client's desire not to experience anger?

- Considering your culture and belief in the divine (e.g., religion, spirituality, agnosticism, atheism), how would your culture and belief system affect how you make sense of the scenario? (See Chapter 13 on speaking about religion.)

- How would the client's culture and religion impact how you make sense of this scenario?

- From your perspective, what would be a therapeutic response to the client?

Scenario 5

A new client says she's just discovered that her husband has been having an affair. He has given this new person 20 years' worth of savings that he and his wife had earmarked for their kids' college expenses and to cover their own living expenses when they retire.

This other person has suddenly fled the country, and now her husband wants to continue his life with your client "as it used to be." Your client says to you, "My priest tells me that God has joined us in holy matrimony, that I must put away all unworthy feelings like anger, that I must love, forgive, and support my husband." She continues, "I'm deeply religious and want to do as my priest says, but I am filled with rage. I am so angry about what my husband did to the kids and me. I need to get rid of this anger." She ends with, "Please help me. I know I must forgive."

- What do you feel as you read this scenario?
- What statements or questions do you think might be most therapeutic?
- What would you like to say to this client?
- What do you think you would say if it is different from what you would like to say?

It may be helpful to remember Maya Angelou's words as we begin to break the myths and acknowledge the power of anger. She stated, "So use that anger, yes, you write it. You paint it, you dance it, you march it, you vote it, you do everything about it. You talk it. Never stop talking it" (Berlinger, 2006, 20:35). As therapists, supervisors, and consultants, let's keep breaking the silence.

11 TALKING ABOUT OPPRESSION

Oppression dehumanizes, and it's a topic that isn't easy to discuss. At its core, *oppression* is a power imbalance between social groups driven by implicit or explicit beliefs that some groups are superior to others (Quiñones-Rosado, 2007, 2020; see also Comas-Díaz, 2021; Frye, 2019; Simon et al., 2022). Examples of oppression include racism (the subject of the next chapter), nativism, ethnocentrism, sexism, heterosexism, cissexism, ableism, ageism, anti-Semitism, and anti-Muslim, which result in cruel, unjust, and marginalizing actions toward individuals, families, and communities. Quiñones-Rosado (2007) described his own journey of realizing his different positions, depending on which context he was focusing on:

> Initially, I focused my analysis of oppression strictly on race and class, and later on culture and nationality, not surprisingly, identities in which I have subordinated status. Eventually, my awareness of the nature of my own relationship to women and to other men also increased, as did my need to change deeply engrained ideas, beliefs, values, and behaviors regarding issues of gender and sexuality in general. I'm still working at it. (p. xix)

https://doi.org/10.1037/0000350-012
Speaking the Unspoken: Breaking the Silence, Myths, and Taboos That Hurt Therapists and Patients, by K. S. Pope, N. Y. Chavez-Dueñas, H. Y. Adames, J. L. Sonne, and B. A. Greene

The vicious ideology and practice of oppression benefits those with power, privilege, and status. It causes deprivation, exclusion, discrimination, exploitation, control, and violence for groups that lack those attributes (G. Nelson & Prilleltensky, 2010). For example, in North American society, White, male, heterosexual, cisgender, Christian, or nondisabled people tend to possess more power, privilege, and status and enjoy their benefits (see Helms, 2016).

The evil nature of institutional oppression and oppressive systems is that oppression is inflicted *even if no one* within the institution or system intends to oppress or commit an intentionally unjust act. All the teachers and administrators in a hypothetical school may hate oppression and want to eliminate it. In a hypothetical court system, all the lawyers and judges may have dedicated their lives to opposing oppression. But if the school uses standardized tests that are biased against one or more groups, or if the court makes sentencing decisions based on standardized tests (e.g., violence prediction) that are similarly biased, then oppression is visited upon the vulnerable.

A crucial question is: Who is responsible for the oppression? We believe everyone who participates in the oppressive system is accountable and bears an inescapable ethical duty to oppose the system's oppression and try to eliminate it by changing how the system or institution functions. In the therapy context, oppression may show up in multiple ways. Consider the following examples:

- You are working at an outpatient clinic where most White patients are receiving individual psychotherapy, but most Patients of Color are receiving medication only or group therapy.

- Imagine yourself working in a clinic where more than half of the clients are monolingual Spanish speakers, but there is only one clinician who speaks Spanish. The clinician is a graduate student completing their practicum under the supervision of a non-Spanish-speaking supervisor.

- A new client has been assigned to you. As you review their chart, you read that the client uses hate speech in therapy to refer to LGBTQIA+ (lesbian, gay, bisexual, transgender, questioning or queer, intersex, asexual, and other forms of sexual and gender identities and orientation) people.

- While watching a supervision video, you observe a male graduate trainee saying the following to his client: "It's okay to be upset at what happened at your job. I get why you yelled at your coworker. Women are emotional by nature."

Each of these four examples confronts us with the subtle ways oppression is baked into the systems in which we work and illustrates how oppression may show up in our work as therapists. We can begin by reflecting on these questions:

- What do the examples invoke in you?
- How might you navigate each scenario?
- What do you envision yourself doing, if anything at all, in each case?
- What impulses, if any, did you experience to keep quiet?
- What would happen if the skilled, resourceful, and persuasive head of the clinic tries to convince you that any thoughts you have about any of those scenarios suggesting that something is amiss (euphemistically had room for improvement) were completely wrong?

Scholars have written about addressing oppression in therapy. For example, Pope et al. (2021) introduced and described the Socialization and Oppression in Psychotherapy Framework (SOP), which describes ways for therapists to navigate moments when a client uses hate speech or other oppressive ideologies in therapy. The SOP outlines five key actions:

a. pause and pay attention to your emotional reactions
b. contextualize the exchange
c. decide how best to proceed
d. take care of your wellness, and
e. consider consultation. (Pope et al., 2021, pp. 298–300)

Several new therapeutic frameworks that focus on supporting clients who are oppressed have begun to emerge. Examples include the keeping radical healing in mind therapeutic approach (Adames et al., 2022), the HEART Framework (Healing Ethno-Racial Trauma Framework; Chavez-Dueñas et al., 2019), the Intersectionality Awakening Model of Womanista (Chavez-Dueñas & Adames, 2021), ethnopolitical psychology (Comas-Díaz, 2007), and womanist and *mujerista* psychologies (Bryant-Davis & Comas-Díaz, 2016).

Addressing oppression in our work as therapists requires that we start talking about it. This chapter focuses on the various forms and levels of oppression and discusses how the topic is complicated yet imperative.

MULTIPLE AND INTERCONNECTED FORMS OF OPPRESSION

Oppression is multidimensional. People can simultaneously be members of social groups that (a) hold power and experience oppression (e.g., a White lesbian cisgender woman) and (b) experience numerous forms of oppression (e.g., Indigenous undocumented immigrant woman with a disability). *Intersectionality*, a theory created and introduced by Black queer women and Black feminist activists and scholars, is a framework that helps name and reveal how oppressive systems interconnect and produce unique forms of inequities (Collins, 2000; Combahee River Collective, 1995; Crenshaw, 1991; Homan et al., 2021; Lewis et al., 2017).

Figure 11.1, developed by Adames et al. (2018), provides a visual model of intersectionality in psychotherapy that can be used to conceptualize clients. It illustrates the intrapsychic (e.g., inside people's minds) and interpsychic

FIGURE 11.1. Visual Model of Intersectionality in Psychotherapy

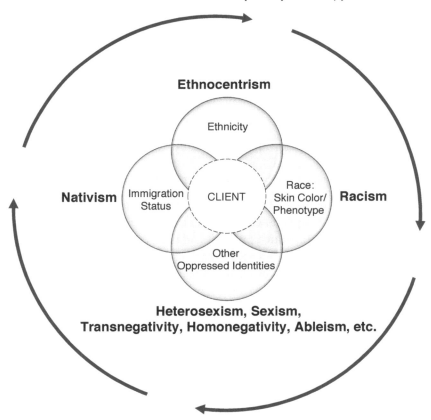

Note. Reprinted from "Intersectionality in Psychotherapy: The Experiences of an AfroLatinx Queer Immigrant," by H. Y. Adames, N. Y. Chavez-Dueñas, S. Sharma, and M. J. La Roche, 2018, *Psychotherapy, 55*(1), p. 75 (https://doi.org/10.1037/pst0000152). Copyright 2018 by the American Psychological Association.

(e.g., occurring between two or more people and between their minds) life of people in context. The model's interconnected inner circles represent our intrapsychic lives and identities. The words outside the circles show the multiple, corresponding interconnected forms of oppression people are likely to experience as a result of belonging to the various social groups. The outer cyclical arrows symbolize the importance of how different forms of oppression and discrimination are likely to shift, depending on context (e.g., school, work, neighborhood, country of origin).

LEVELS OF OPPRESSION

Three main levels of oppression are (a) institutional, (b) interpersonal, and (c) internalized. Institutional oppression does not require an identified perpetrator. As Florynce Kennedy (1970) wrote, "Where a system of oppression has become institutionalized, it is unnecessary for individuals to be oppressive" (p. 439). *Institutional oppression* is a system of laws, policies, and practices that exclude and deny opportunities and access to resources for people from various minoritized social groups (C. P. Jones, 2000; J. M. Jones, 1972; S. C. Jones & Neblett, 2019; Moise & Hankerson, 2021).

Interpersonal oppression requires an identifiable perpetrator. It consists of individual acts of discrimination and dehumanization carried out by a member of a social group with more power in society against someone with less power when compared with the perpetrator.

Internalized oppression results when a member of a minoritized group accepts and believes the negative messages about their group and experiences feelings of self-doubt and disgust for themselves and the members of their group (see Pyke, 2010). Individuals with internalized oppression operate according to the damaging stereotypes, values, images, and ideologies perpetrated by the social group with power. This form of oppression includes internalized racism, internalized heterosexism, internalized sexism, internalized ableism, internalized ageism, internalized anti-Semitism, internalized anti-Muslims, and the like.

REFLECTING ON OPPRESSION

Talking about oppression is hard. The topic is emotionally loaded and often makes us uncomfortable. Many of us also come from training programs in which deep discussions about oppression were neither prioritized nor modeled. Traditionally, the topic of oppression, for example, is often not framed as an ethical imperative for our work as therapists. In turn, we may not see the value of addressing oppression in psychotherapy (see Pope et al., 2021). Unsurprisingly, many of us avoid talking openly and candidly about oppression.

On the few occasions when oppression is discussed, the conversation often stays at the superficial or abstract level (e.g., intellectualizing). Other times, we may focus on the interpersonal level of oppression while ignoring the impact of systemic (e.g., police brutality, health disparities, racism-related stress, trauma) and internalized oppression (e.g., Clients of Color viewing people with white skin as more beautiful and resorting to using skin-bleaching creams, a queer client seeking conversion therapy). Although the focus on interpersonal oppression may appear coincidental, it may reflect something entirely different, although not always conscious. The interpersonal focus serves as a strategy of power evasion that helps minimize feelings of discomfort, such as guilt that comes from being the recipient of unearned systemic advantages (i.e., privilege; see Frankenberg, 1997; Hazelbaker & Mistry, 2022; Neville et al., 2013). It reflects the belief that oppression is a problem solely between individuals because everyone reportedly has the same opportunities despite existing differences within a society.

QUESTIONS FOR REFLECTION AND DISCUSSION

The following questions—some of which follow scenarios—help us to reflect more deeply and speak more openly about the roles of all three levels of oppression in our lives, work, and society. This exercise enables us to address oppression and its effects more realistically and effectively with our clients.

Exercise: Assessing Current Foundational Knowledge

Before we begin discussing oppression with others, we need to have some foundational knowledge about the subject. The following questions can help us reflect on how much we know about oppression:

- As you read the preceding section, Reflecting on Oppression, what came to mind?
- Did you find yourself thinking, "This all sounds familiar" or "I already know this material"?
- Are you wondering, "What does all this have to do with psychotherapy?"
- Is there a part of you that says, "What a load of crap!"?

Perhaps you thought, "I had not thought about oppression in this way," or "Much of this information is fairly new to me." Before being ready to discuss oppression with clients, it is essential to determine how to fill any knowledge gaps by completing additional readings and getting the necessary training to enhance your competence in this area (see Adams et al., 2018; Alvarez et al., 2016; Andrews, 2020; Chavez-Dueñas et al., 2019; David & Derthick, 2018; Nakamura & Logie, 2020; T. D. Nelson, 2017; Pope et al., 2021).

Exercise: Our Personal Experiences With Oppression—Self Exploration

We now invite you to engage in self-exploration about your experiences with oppression. Take as much time as you need. Consider completing the following questions with one or more people:

- What are your immediate reactions when oppression is mentioned?

- Do you find yourself wishing the topic was not mentioned? Do you prefer avoiding the topic or wondering why the subject of oppression matters to the discussion at hand?

- What forms of oppression have you experienced?

- How has oppression impacted your life?

- In what ways might you have been a perpetrator of oppression against others?

- How might you have benefited from the oppression of others? How do you make sense of this experience?

Exercise: Breaking the Silence on Our Adjustment to Oppression

Central themes in this book are the personal and social challenges we encounter when talking about taboo topics. Part of breaking the silence includes having difficult and honest conversations that require us to be vulnerable and create ways to tap into our courage. West (2008) reminded us that

> it takes courage to look in the mirror and see who you really are when you take off the mask when you are not performing the same old routines and social roles. It takes courage to ask—how did I become so well-adjusted to injustice? (p. 8)

To continue the journey toward breaking the silence on oppression, consider the following three questions proposed by Parham at the 2017 Teachers College, Columbia University, Winter Roundtable:

- What allows you to bear witness to the suffering and pain of the oppressed, sit in silence, and still maintain your humanity?

- What keeps you caught in a space where you feel paralyzed about being able to make a change about the pain caused by oppression?

- What does integrity look like for you in the face of oppression? (T. A. Parham, personal communication, October 20, 2022; see also Parham & Sue, 2017)

Exercise: Talking About Oppression in Therapy

Oppression impacts the well-being of minoritized individuals and groups. We need to develop ways to address and name oppression in all its forms in our work. Creating opportunities or welcoming curiosity in therapy about how oppression may contribute to or exacerbate the client's symptoms can be validating and valuable for the therapeutic process. See Adames et al. (2022) and Pope et al. (2021) for further discussions on developing ways to address oppression in psychotherapy. Consider the scenarios that follow.

Scenario 1

You're working with a new client. As you're preparing to see them, you review their prior psychotherapy records and read that the client has a history of being "provocative" in therapy. The previous therapist describes the client as using derogatory speech toward People of Color, transgender people, and other minoritized groups in therapy.

- What does the scenario evoke in you?

- What are some of the challenges you foresee working with this client?

- What image comes to mind when you try to picture who the client is?

- What reactions do you experience when envisioning the client as being a White cisgender heterosexual male?
  - What if the client is an Asian cisgender lesbian?
  - Let's say the client is an older adult?
  - What if they are a teenager?
  - What if the client reflects your social group membership?

- Have you experienced someone using derogatory language to refer to you? Has anyone called you a slur?

- How do you think that may play out in this scenario?

- Have you used or thought of using offensive language toward someone of a minoritized group at any time in your life? How might those experiences or practices impact your work with this client?

Scenario 2

You're working with an undocumented Muslim immigrant. Sessions often start with the client's discussing being frustrated and feeling empty and out of place at work and college. Lately, they've experienced being angrier and think that "no one understands" them. They state, "I really work hard to be a good citizen. I guess I need to do better."

- What does the scenario evoke in you?

- What are some of the challenges you foresee working with this client?

- How would you respond to the client's report that "no one understands" them?

- How might you contribute to the client's experiences of not feeling understood and seen as a hardworking person? Do you consider yourself part of the "no one" in the client's life?

- When clients spontaneously bring up the topic of oppression in therapy, it is essential to listen, validate their experiences, and discuss how such experiences may be contributing to their distress. What part would be challenging for you to validate? What contributes to the challenge?

- Do you think helping the client relinquish the anger would be therapeutic and helpful? If so, what oppressive message might you be giving the client if you focus on anger management?

- In what ways is the client blaming themselves (internalizing the oppression)?

Exercise: When the Therapist Oppresses

The conundrum about oppression in psychotherapy is that we, as therapists, are not immune to oppressing our clients, however unintentionally. Pope et al. (2021) provided four examples of how therapists can be oppressive in therapy:

> (a) using offensive language, (b) invalidating or minimizing clients' experiences and narratives of oppression, (c) silencing or ignoring clients' attempts to share the experiences of oppression and its impact in their lives, and (d) taking too much space in therapy and centering ourselves when the client discusses experiences of oppression and dehumanization. (p. 300)

To help break the silence about oppression in therapy, consider the following questions:

- Do you want to rescue your clients when they're sharing experiences of oppression?

- In what ways might you have silenced, minimized, or ignored your clients' attempts to discuss how they've been harmed by oppression?

- How do you navigate your anxiety and distress when oppression is discussed in therapy?

- Having gone through all of the exercises in this section, what might you need to do differently to talk openly and honestly about oppression with yourself, clients, supervisees, supervisors, and colleagues?

- What reactions are you noticing as you respond to these questions?

We invite you to continue reflecting on and talking about oppression. Come back from time to time to the exercises and questions in this chapter; ask others to join you in exploring the taboo subject. And, again, we welcome you to defy moving away from the topic of oppression that, as we've described, is one that isn't easy to discuss. But together we can help eliminate systems of oppression and their dehumanizing force.

12 SPEAKING UP ABOUT WHITE SUPREMACY CULTURE

The concept of *race*, an imprecise and made-up category used to describe and group people based on phenotype, continues to create dehumanizing conditions for People of Color across the globe. White people used the separation of people based on race to assign unearned advantages (i.e., privilege) and superiority status to people in the White group. Individuals deemed non-White were described as inferior and were systematically disadvantaged. This ideology is the foundation of White supremacy, which we typically associate with explicitly racist, extremist individuals and groups, such as White nationalists and the Ku Klux Klan (i.e., White supremacists).

However, White supremacy goes beyond these extreme individualistic examples. It also includes the *culture* of White supremacy, which refers to the economic and political systems that promote dominance of people who are racially White (Adames et al., 2021; Grzanka et al., 2019; Helms, 2017). White supremacy culture reflects such problems as racial health disparities, segregation in housing, and a racial wealth gap. Okun (2021) wrote the following:

> White supremacy culture is reflected in the current realities of disproportionate and systemic **harm and violence** directed towards BIPOC [Black, Indigenous, and other People of Color] people and communities in all aspects of our national life—health, education, employment, incarceration, policing, the law,

https://doi.org/10.1037/0000350-013
Speaking the Unspoken: Breaking the Silence, Myths, and Taboos That Hurt Therapists and Patients, by K. S. Pope, N. Y. Chavez-Dueñas, H. Y. Adames, J. L. Sonne, and B. A. Greene

the environment, immigration, agriculture, food, housing. We would not allow any of the ways in which our society prioritizes profit over people if we did not have dominant cultural beliefs that make normal what is deeply and alarmingly inhumane. (para. 18)

Our professional ethics and life-affirming stance help us reject the culture of White supremacy (Pope et al., 2021). Denouncing White supremacy culture and racial hatred is often easy. However, our training programs, conferences, and professional associations need to create opportunities to explore how White dominance affects our profession, our educational institutions, our theories and research, our work, and our day-to-day lives (Adames et al., 2021). White supremacy culture dictates not only how society is structured but also who holds power—what Nobles (n.d.) described as "the ability to define reality and to have others respond to your definition as if it were your own" (para. 2). Helms (2008) noted that "White people have the power to designate which physical similarities among people are 'racial,' what racial label should be assigned to them, and who has the power to count categories and make laws and policies pertaining to them" (pp. 1–2).

The culture of White supremacy may show up in the work we do as therapists in nuanced ways. Examples include the following: having People of Color wait longer on wait-lists, using treatment modalities that fail to address cultural differences, minimizing or invalidating a client's experiences of racism and oppression, assigning Clients of Color to less experienced clinicians or giving them medications instead of psychotherapy, or pathologizing behaviors that are culturally appropriate (e.g., emotional vitality; indirect forms of communication; *healthy cultural suspicion*, which refers to being cautious about trusting the system).

Consider this clinical exchange: A Client of Color shares an incident that occurred over the weekend while they helped move their nephew to college. After dinner, the client and their family went to a local coffee shop to buy tea and mugs for their nephew. The client described feeling angry after the cashier threw the credit card on the counter and did not pack the mugs. The client then proceeded to ask for a bag, and, again, the cashier threw the bag and walked away. Listening attentively, the therapist says, "Sorry you experienced such treatment. It sounds like the cashier was having a bad day." The client responds, "Nope, I don't think she was having a bad day. She responded to me that way because of my accent." The therapist replies, "Wondering if she was in a rush. Was there a long line in the store?" The client says, "It was pretty empty. I think we were treated like crap because we aren't White."

- What are your emotional reactions as you read the clinical exchange?
- How might the therapist's response invalidate or minimize the client's experience?

- What are some ways the therapist is silencing or ignoring the client's attempts to process their recent experience of oppression?
- How might the therapist's response affect the therapeutic relationship, and how may it impact what the client shares in the future?

The ideology and culture of White supremacy create *racism*, the interpersonal, institutional, and cultural oppression of groups of people based on the belief in racial superiority (Helms, 2008; J. M. Jones, 1997). Although "race" is a socially invented category, "racism" has real-life social, political, educational, economic, and health consequences for People of Color. We must resist denying and minimizing its existence and begin speaking up about it (see Adames & Chavez-Dueñas, 2017; Alvarez et al., 2016; Smedley & Smedley, 2005).

SPEAKING UP ABOUT RACISM AND WHITE SUPREMACY CULTURE

Talking about White supremacy culture requires us to acknowledge these topics and notice the emotions, thoughts, and other reactions they evoke. Some of us may experience guilt, shame, anxiety, confusion, or sweaty palms. Others may experience frustration, sadness, hopelessness, confusion, or a need for affirmation. Still others may feel resentment, irritation, anger, aggression, or a sense of being attacked or put on the defensive, of people "playing the race card" or "acting like a victim." And some may yawn with boredom, indifference, and an eagerness to move on to other topics. (What do you yourself experience?) In these moments, we may wonder whether we and the other people in the discussion are operating according to the same terms or struggling to find words to communicate our subjectivities. We may look for signs of connection and misalignment as we listen and respond to each other.

Our feelings may grow stronger if we begin to conclude that we are talking with others who may have different experiences and views about racism and Whiteness. Questions may quickly surface: "Is this conversation even worth it?" "What am I going to get out of talking to someone who just doesn't get it?" "Ugh, do I have the energy for this right now?"

Our lack of formal training and experience discussing Whiteness and racism only adds to the challenge of speaking up on the topic. We often confront situations that require us to decide whether to speak up or to stay silent about racism and White supremacy culture. Consider the following two scenarios.

Scenario 1

A couple who is White has been planning their anniversary celebration for several months. The plan includes going to the theater and having dinner at the new five-star restaurant in town. Getting reservations at this restaurant is a challenge. When they called, the host explained that several tables were reserved for walk-ins.

On the night of the anniversary, the couple arrives early to the restaurant. While waiting to check in with the host, they see an older, African American couple waiting in line. The host tells that couple that all tables are taken and they'll need to make a reservation if they want to eat there. Hearing this information and thinking they are out of luck, the couple who is White begins to walk away but then decide they've got nothing to lose by asking about the first-come, first served tables. The host says, "Oh, yes, we have three walk-in tables available by the bar. Follow me."

- What would you do if you found yourself in this situation?
- Would you take the table?
- Would you say something or would you stay quiet?
- If you decide to speak up, what would you say?
- Have you ever been in a position similar to the Black couple waiting in line?

Scenario 2

Last year, you joined a weekly consultation group for your group practice via Zoom. The group comprises two White male clinicians (Tony and Mark), two White female clinicians (Amy and Becky), a Black female clinician (Zuri), a Latinx male clinician (Carlos), and you. You view yourself as having a good, collaborative relationship with all members and feel that the consultation has been helpful for your practice and professional development.

At the last meeting, the first in person in more than a year, Zuri, said she would no longer attend the group meetings and thanked everyone for allowing her to join the group. As Zuri begins to stand up to leave, Carlos says he is not coming back, either. Amy asks, "What happened?" Zuri states, "It's complicated, but I don't have time to get into it right now." Carlos adds, "Honestly, we are both tired of being put in a position where we have to teach you stuff constantly you should already know. You are constantly making offensive comments. We don't have the energy for all that."

- What are your initial reactions to this scenario?
- What are some things you would consider?
- How would you make sense of what is happening?
- How do you envision yourself responding, if at all?
- To what degree, if at all, would you feel defensive?

QUESTIONS FOR REFLECTION AND DISCUSSION

These following questions help us (a) assess our current and past reactions to topics about racism and White supremacy culture and (b) strengthen our ability to engage to speak openly, honestly, and directly about these topics.

Exercise: Observe Your Emotional Reaction

What are some of your emotional reactions when the topic of racism and White supremacy culture are mentioned?

Exercise: Review Past Experiences

Think back to a time when you were talking with someone or in a group and the subject of racism or White privilege was brought up.

- Were you an active participant in the discussion?
- Did you help deflect, disrupt, or undermine the conversation?
- Did apprehension and uncertainty about how to engage in the dialogue hijack your actions?
- Did those two topics seem like "much ado about nothing"—that too much time and attention are devoted to them?
- Did the discussion seem to represent a political or ideological agenda that you disagree with?
- Did it seem like the purpose of the discussion was to attack and shame White people and to accuse them all of racism?
- If you were to find yourself in a similar situation again, what do you think you would need to become an active participant in the discussion?

Exercise: Explore Barriers to Speaking Up

When you have witnessed instances of racism or racial injustice, do you tend to speak up, or do you take on the role of a bystander and stay silent? If you tend to remain quiet, what motivates your silence?

Do any of the statements that follow sound familiar?

- This is not an issue that is significant enough for me to speak up about.
- I don't have the time or energy to engage in race talks with others.
- I have too much to lose, and I am not willing to risk it if I speak up.
- I'm afraid whatever I do will only make things worse.
- I want to speak up, but I don't know what to do or say.

- I am too anxious to speak up.
- I don't want to say the wrong thing.
- I am worried about what others in the group will think of me if I speak up.
- I am worried about my safety if I say what's really on my mind.

IT MAY NOT GET EASIER, BUT WE CAN GET BETTER WITH PRACTICE

It is critical to identify roadblocks that may stop us from speaking up about racism and White supremacy culture. One roadblock is that we may expect that speaking up will get easier with experience, and then it does not. It's helpful to take a different approach. It may not get easier, but we can get better.

Keeping the following three principles in mind can help us dismantle this roadblock:

- Speaking about racism and White supremacy culture will never be easy; this is not the goal. Instead, the goal is to resist the fantasy that speaking up about race, racism, and Whiteness comes without uncomfortable feelings and awkward moments.

- The more we proactively create spaces to talk about racism or engage in the discussion when it comes up in conversation, the better we'll get at navigating the emotions the topics evoke. We'll also release the expectation of not making mistakes and instead accept that errors are part of the process of learning, growing, and repairing.

- If we intend to and want to strengthen our ability to speak up about these issues but need more training and experience to do it, we can consider how best to fill in these gaps (e.g., webinars, presentations, readings on the topic, consultation).

Suppose we find ourselves disengaged from the topic of racism, oppression, and White Supremacy culture. Or we begin to think that talking about the topic is not all that important, is maybe a complete waste of time, and is a distraction from the basics of psychotherapy that we want to learn about. If this is the case, it may be important to consider what having this lack of interest in the topics means for us and how it may impact our work as a therapist, especially when considering our ethics of doing no harm.

Let's keep talking!

13 TALKING ABOUT RELIGION

Religion can show up in therapy in nuanced and unexpected ways. Conversations about religion have a legitimate place in the psychotherapeutic process. Consider the following four hypothetical vignettes.

VIGNETTE 1

During your first session with a new psychotherapy client, they tell you that religion is central to their life and they do not believe anyone who is not a believer can truly understand them or be helpful. They ask what your religious beliefs, if any, are.

- What are your thoughts and feelings when you hear this question?
- In what different ways do you consider responding?
- What do you believe would be the best way to respond?

https://doi.org/10.1037/0000350-014
Speaking the Unspoken: Breaking the Silence, Myths, and Taboos That Hurt Therapists and Patients, by K. S. Pope, N. Y. Chavez-Dueñas, H. Y. Adames, J. L. Sonne, and B. A. Greene

VIGNETTE 2

During the intake session, a woman tells you she has come to you for therapy to help her find ways to accept her daily responsibilities, such as cleaning the house, buying groceries, cooking, filling the car with gas, and so on. You say you believe you can work with her on those issues and invite her to tell you more specifically what she's finding challenging. The client says that she and her husband belong to a religious denomination that believes women must accept the man's role as head of the family. The client's husband tells her when and what she must do. He also tells her she has to please him sexually by doing things she experiences as uncomfortable. They had a counseling session as a couple with their clergy who told her it was sinful for her to question her husband's authority and that she must find ways to obey. So, she is coming to you for help in obeying her husband.

- What are your thoughts and feelings as you put yourself in the place of this therapist?
- What different ways do you consider responding?
- What do you believe would be the best way to respond?

VIGNETTE 3

You're supervising a therapist who believes it is unethical to provide any treatment that is not scientifically supported by empirical research. The supervisee's new client is deeply religious and believes everything that happens is according to a divine plan and ordained by God's will. The supervisee describes to you how they are using CBT (cognitive behavior therapy) to identify and replace what the supervisee terms "unfounded cognitions that are self-defeating for the client," undermining the client's sense of agency.

- What thoughts and feelings occur to you as you put yourself in the place of this supervisor?
- What would be your primary goal during the supervision session?
- What would be the first thing you would say to the supervisee?

VIGNETTE 4

You're supervising a graduate student assigned to provide therapy to a woman who identified herself in the first session as a lesbian. The student describes to you how they ended the session at that point: The student told the patient that because of their own devoutly held religious beliefs, they cannot provide professional services of any kind to people who are LGBTQIA+ (lesbian, gay, bisexual, transgender, questioning or queer, intersex, asexual, and other forms of sexual and gender identities and orientation), including referring to other therapists.

- What thoughts and feelings come up for you as you put yourself in the place of this supervisor?
- What would be your primary goal during the supervision session?
- What would be the first thing you would say to the supervisee?

HOW WE TALK–OR REMAIN SILENT–ABOUT RELIGION

The familiar American rule of etiquette, "Do not discuss religion or politics in general company," first appeared in print in the late 19th century (Chrisman, 2015, p. 130). The primary rationale for the rule is that these twin topics typically triggered discord and unhappiness in social gatherings. The rule may be pretty old, but we still tend to avoid mentioning them in most settings unless the setting is one in which everyone shares (or is assumed to share) our beliefs. In this chapter, we focus on the silence around the topic of religion. According to the Pew Research Center (2019b), most Americans report that they do not discuss religion either with family members or with others on a regular basis (see also Pew Research Center, 2019a). Not surprisingly, psychotherapists are no different. Research findings indicate that even when we acknowledge the importance of the topic, we often fail to speak with clients about religion (Frazier & Hansen, 2009; Hathaway et al., 2004).

Vast differences in perspectives on the topic of religion have not helped. For instance, to some, the Christian Christmas holiday is inflicted on everyone, like it or not, through seemingly omnipresent music playing in stores decked out in Christmas-themed decorations, television programming, and strangers wishing them "Merry Christmas." To others, however, evil Scrooges have banished virtually all traces of traditional Christmas, replacing them with generic secular sentiments like "Happy Holidays" through a heartless "War on Christmas" (see Bowler & Bowler, 2017; J. Gibson, 2006; Hodge, 2013; D. K. Johnson, 2013; Joshi, 2020; Smith, 2018).

Fear, hatred, rejection, and lack of understanding of those who worship— or of individuals assumed to worship—in certain religious traditions have also hurt our ability to talk with each other openly, honestly, and respectfully about religion. These negative reactions to some religions are not just individual challenges; they are systemic problems that have a long history in the

United States. For instance, Native Americans were prevented from freely practicing their religion until 1978, and African religions, such as Santeria, Voodoo, and Candomblé, are often portrayed as superstitious and deviant (Bartkowski, 1998; Mbiti, 1991; Native American Rights Fund, 1979). More recently, the deadly attack on civilians during 9/11 sparked widespread fear and hatred of Muslims and those thought to be Muslim, leading to discrimination, covert surveillance, and attacks (Bayoumi, 2015; Gerteis et al., 2020; Love, 2017; Selod, 2019). In 2015, the candidate who would win the U.S. presidency campaigned on a promise to enact a "total and complete shutdown of Muslims entering the United States" (J. Johnson, 2015, para. 1). Even more recently,

> anti-Muslim sentiment has spiked. . . . Existing and proposed mosque sites across the country have been targeted for vandalism and other criminal acts, and there have been efforts to block or deny necessary zoning permits for the construction and expansion of other facilities. (American Civil Liberties Union, 2022, para. 1)

Attacks on houses of worship in the U.S. are not rare or limited to those in which Muslims worship. In 2019, for example, Reuters (2019) described "9 Recent Attacks at U.S. Houses of Worship." They included

- an armed man storming the Chabad of Poway synagogue in San Diego, California, shooting one worshipper who died and injuring three others;

- a man shooting and killing four people and injuring five others at the New Life Church in Colorado Springs, Colorado, and a Christian missionary training center 70 miles away;

- a man shooting and killing two people and wounding seven others at the Tennessee Valley Unitarian Church in Knoxville, Tennessee;

- a man shooting and killing six people and wounding three others at the Sikh Temple of Wisconsin in Oak Creek;

- a man shooting and killing nine worshippers as they prayed in the Emanuel African Methodist Episcopal Church in Charleston, South Carolina;

- a man shooting and wounding six people as they worshipped in the Burnette Chapel Church of Christ in Nashville, Tennessee;

- a man opening fire with a gun and killing 26 worshippers as they prayed in the First Baptist Church in Sutherland Springs, Texas;

- a man shooting a gun, killing 11 worshippers and wounding six others, including Holocaust survivors, at the Tree of Life synagogue in Pittsburgh, Pennsylvania; and

- a man burning down three Black churches in Southern Louisiana within the span of 10 days.

Within this context, it is perhaps no wonder that religion has, for decades, tended to be a difficult topic to raise and discuss in a direct, authentic, and, most of all, therapeutic way (O. Brown et al., 2013; Schultz-Ross & Gutheil, 1997). The challenge may be complicated by the fact that therapists and clients may not share a vocabulary with which to dialogue about this topic. Surveys suggest that psychologists are significantly less religious than the clients who come to them for help (see Delaney et al., 2007; Magyar-Russell, 2020). There is also confusion around the meaning and relationship of such terms as "religion," "spirituality," "faith," and "sacred." K. A. Harris et al. (2018) conducted three content analyses of publications that spanned a 30-year period. Based on the results, they proposed that

> spirituality is a search for or relationship with the sacred; religiousness is ritual, institutional, or codified spirituality which is culturally sanctioned; faith is a synonym for spirituality and/or religiousness; and the sacred is manifestations of the divine, existential meaningfulness, or an ultimate concern as perceived by an individual. (p. 1)

Many of us may also wonder if we are meeting the ethical responsibility of competent practice when religion becomes a critical issue in therapy but we are relatively uninformed about the client's faith, or we may have biases about the religion they practice.

QUESTIONS FOR REFLECTION AND DISCUSSION

The following sets of questions—each set keyed to a particular theme—can help us think more clearly and speak more openly, honestly, and directly about religion.

Exercise: Religion in General

- How would you describe the role and importance of religion in your life, if it has a role and importance?
  - If religion has a significant role in your life, how public is your religious affiliation?
  - If it is public, how would you react if a client told you that they know you practice a particular faith?
  - If religion has a significant role in your life, how would you react if a client talked disparagingly about your faith?
- Are there any religions that you dislike?

- Are there any religions you are afraid of? If so, what specifically causes your fear?

- Do you believe that religious beliefs are compatible with a scientific understanding of the universe?

- How, if at all, has any religion done something good for people or been a force for good in the world?

- How, if at all, has any religion harmed people or been a hurtful or destructive force?

- In your training, was the topic of religion ever discussed?
    - If so, in what context (e.g., didactic course, supervision)?
    - What was your experience?

- Imagine a client tells you that they practice a religion that you know nothing about.
    - What are your feelings and thoughts?
    - How would you proceed with the client? Would you consider transferring the client? Why or why not?

- Imagine a client asked you to pray with them.
    - What are your feelings and thoughts?
    - How would you decide to respond to their request?

- Imagine a client asked you to pray for them.
    - What are your feelings and thoughts?
    - How would you choose to respond to their request?

Exercise: Nonbelievers and Religiously Unaffiliated People

Although many people in the United States practice religion, not everyone has a religious faith. Atheism and agnosticism also are topics American society does not make easy for people to discuss. Broadly, *atheism* is defined as an absence of belief in the existence of any god or deities. *Agnosticism* is the view that it is practically impossible to know with certainty whether any gods exist. At their core, agonistic people do not commit to believing in the existence or nonexistence of gods. A survey conducted by the Pew Research Center (2019b) found that 4% of adults in the United States identified as atheists and 5%, as agnostics, in 2018 and 2019, a significant increase compared with 2% atheists and 3% agnostics in 2009. Another 17% of those surveyed described their religion as "nothing in particular," which also increased from 12% in 2009.

Atheist and agnostic people in the United States, and to some degree across the globe, are discriminated against for being nonbelievers or religiously unaffiliated people. Nonbelievers in god are often described as dishonest, deviant, angry, and self-indulgent (see Brewster et al., 2020; Gervais et al., 2011; Saroglou et al., 2011). In the development and evaluation of a psychological instrument to examine minority stress experiences of nonbelievers, titled Measure of Atheist Discrimination Experiences, Brewster et al. (2016) noted that,

> overwhelmingly, national survey data supports that Americans have significant bias against atheist people. . . . Some of this bias may stem from beliefs that atheist people are different or deviant; indeed, data suggest that people in the United States view atheists as the social group (other groups included Muslims, immigrants, and sexual minority individuals) *least likely* to share their vision of American society (Edgell et al., 2006). These beliefs may translate to actions that marginalize atheist people in their daily lives; for example . . . Americans report that they would be least accepting of their son or daughter marrying an atheist compared to someone from another religious group (Edgell et al., 2006) . . . Americans would be least likely to vote for an atheist in a Presidential election out of all other religious group memberships (McCarthy, 2015). . . . Atheists report high levels of discrimination in schools, at places of employment, within the legal system, and across many other community and social settings. (pp. 557–558)

We hope the following exercises encourage honest and sincere dialogues on atheism and agnosticism as topics we can discuss in our training and practice.

- Do you identify as an atheist, agnostic, or nonbeliever? If so:
  - Have you experienced pressure to pass as a religious person?
  - How did you navigate those experiences?
  - What are your emotional reactions as you think about your experiences as an atheist, agnostic, or nonbeliever?
  - What may be supporting or hindering you from openly talking about your atheism or agnosticism?
  - Are those reasons present with the person or group you're completing this exercise with?
  - Are you comfortable discussing your atheist or agnostic views during therapy sessions with your clients? Do you think your views impact your understanding of or help provided to your clients with strong religious beliefs or the sharing of your ideologies with your supervisor?

- If you don't identify as an atheist, agnostic, or a nonbeliever, consider the following:
  - Growing up, what were the messages that you received about people who are nonbelievers?

- Which of these messages do you continue to believe?
- How might this impact your work with clients who identify as atheists or agnostics? What about a religiously unaffiliated supervisor?
- How connected are you to your religion? How secure do you feel in your relationship with your god(s)?
- Do you wear jewelry or have paraphernalia in your office that might communicate your religious affiliation to your clients? If so, how might this impact your work with an atheist or agnostic client?

Exercise: Science, Religion, and Nonbelievers Coexisting

The relationship between science and religion is another twin topic that people avoid. Were you socialized to believe that matters of the heart and subjects of the mind are like oil and water: They can never mix? Can you think of a public figure or someone who believes in science and a higher power in their personal life? Or someone who believes in one but not the other? We can write another book on this topic alone. But staying on topic, how can we build narratives with our clients and others with whom we work that honors the existence of believers, nonbelievers and all the in-betweenness?

Consider the following questions, outlined by Pope et al. (2021):

- How is reality defined? Who defines what is real?
- What are your values? What are your non-negotiables?
- How was the universe created? Is there a higher power? If so, who are they?
- Describe the ways you believe knowledge is created?
- How do you connect and build relationships with others? (p. 77)

Although conversations about religion continue to be fraught with problems in our society, it is likely that this topic will show up in the therapy room. It is essential for us as therapists to have done our job thinking and reflecting about this topic in our personal lives and considering its potential impact on our professional roles. We hope this chapter and the exercises included in it are a step to help you become more comfortable thinking and talking about religion.

14 TALKING ABOUT MONEY AND FEES

Many of us have something in common: We talk about how we don't like talking about money. The dislike for talking about money extends into our work as psychotherapists. Trachtman (2008a) noted that "as a result of this taboo, money issues are seldom addressed either in our professional training or in the psychological literature, and most clinicians tend to avoid exploring (the topic) for themselves or with their clients" (p. 1; see also Yager & Kay, 2022). In this chapter, we focus on money as an underdiscussed topic. We consider the aspect of "money issues" that we likely most often think of in our work: setting, charging, and collecting fees. We also address other, more general, themes related to money as it affects the internal and external lives of our patients and ourselves.

Why is money a taboo topic? Schofield (1971) speculated that "Freud may indeed have been right—that the apparently persistent reticence about fees is a function of shame" (p. 10). Schofield appears prescient in predicting that the growing third-party coverage of psychotherapy would remove some of the discomfort and secrecy from this area. He missed the mark, however, in claiming that third-party coverage would quickly move us toward a "unified structure of fees and payments that will be rational and reasonable, protecting the practitioners and . . . client" (p. 11).

https://doi.org/10.1037/0000350-015
Speaking the Unspoken: Breaking the Silence, Myths, and Taboos That Hurt Therapists and Patients, by K. S. Pope, N. Y. Chavez-Dueñas, H. Y. Adames, J. L. Sonne, and B. A. Greene
Copyright © 2023 by the American Psychological Association. All rights reserved.

Trachtman (2008a, 2008b) noted other potential motives than shame for difficulties discussing money. For example, money is often identified with issues that can raise anxiety and internal conflict: sex, power, competence, security, personal value, pleasure, freedom, and evil.

Mendoza (2021) suggested we may carry within us a stereotype of the "greedy therapist." The five authors of this volume agreed on the following description of this money-obsessed character: They charge more per hour than we collect in a week; they accept only nondemanding, wealthy patients who can easily afford their fees; they believe that volunteering, sliding scales, and pro bono work are character flaws; and they spend their vacations in one of their mansions in some fancy part of the world. Mendoza suggested that whatever internalized image of a greedy therapist we carry, it may sometimes be the focus of self-righteous scorn, condemnation, and persecution (while not so coincidentally distracting us from whatever feelings of shame and guilt we may have about our own desire for wealth). Furthermore, at other times, we may burn with envy, discouraged that this selfish clod who does so much less real work than we do, gets paid much more than we do, never has to worry about paying the bills, and lives in luxury.

Yet we often confront money issues in our work with clients. Most obviously, we face the daunting task of navigating an obstacle course of fees and payment details. Consider the following:

- charging private insurance companies or government programs for patient contacts via phone or video
- working within the limited number of sessions covered by insurance companies
- obtaining copayments
- securing prior authorization
- managing "parity" that exists in legislation but less so in practice
- responding to insurance reviews
- submitting claim forms for insurance reimbursement that are "lost"
- processing reimbursement checks that arrive months late
- dealing with unpaid hours spent on the phone with insurance reps

Other themes related to money fall prey to this avoidance (Trachtman, 2008a, 2011; Yager & Kay, 2022). For example, we continue to overlook—or downright ignore—the internal psychological meaning and importance of money for us personally and for our clients: money-related beliefs, attitudes, and behaviors that impact what we think of ourselves and how we relate to others. Trachtman (2008b) warned that to the extent that the money taboo undermines psychotherapists' ability to understand their own money issues and to explore the issues that affect their patients, it has a negative effect on their therapeutic effectiveness. It is helpful if people are able to communicate thoughts and feelings about money to psycho-therapists, especially when those thoughts and feelings are causing problems in adaptation. (p. 13)

Yager and Kay (2022) wrote,

Evidence suggests that money matters influencing intrapsychic and interpersonal lives commonly cause emotional distress, generating a range of dysfunctional behaviors. These reactions manifest as explicit conflicts, implicit issues, and unequivocal money-related pathologies. Clinical vignettes illustrate specific issues. By explicitly addressing money matters in patient's intrapsychic and interpersonal lives, trainees can enrich their assessments, case formulations, treatment planning, and ongoing psychotherapy. (para. 1)

If we do not pay careful attention to the possible issues of money in our work, we may miss recognizing and exploring the degree to which our clients struggle with the common problem of substantial debt. According to a recent survey by the American Psychological Association (2022a), the stress associ-ated with debt (e.g., credit cards, student and auto loans, hefty mortgages) is at the highest level recorded for American adults since 2015. Debt stress negatively impacts our clients' emotional and physical health; disrupts pri-mary relationships; contributes to increased impulsive behaviors, including substance abuse and compensatory spending; and can compromise decision making (Berger et al., 2016; Dew et al., 2012; Jackson et al., 2016; Richardson et al., 2017; Sharma et al., 2014).

Money remains a sensitive topic for many of us. It throws roadblocks in our way as we try to understand our clients and communicate openly, honestly, and clearly with them as well as with supervisors, clinical consultants, and payment sources (e.g., insurance companies, case reviewers, government programs).

QUESTIONS FOR REFLECTION AND DISCUSSION

Here we offer exercises designed to help us think more clearly and speak more freely about money in our lives and in our work.

- What feelings does your current financial situation evoke in you?
  - Are you ever embarrassed or uneasy that you have either less or more money than others in your circle?
  - Are you ever envious of those who have more money?

- Do you discuss your fees in the first session with a new client, or do you rely on the written information in your informed consent form?
  - If you talk about your fees, how comfortable are you with that discussion?
  - Are there client characteristics or demographics that make the discussion easier? More difficult?
- How do you feel when a client asks you directly if you might reduce your fee?
  - Under what circumstances, if any, are you likely to reduce your fee?
  - Under what circumstances, if any, would you refuse to lower your fee?
  - Do client characteristics or demographics affect your decision?
- Imagine a client who forgets to pay their bill. The first time it happens, would you (a) figure they'd remember next time or (b) remind them?
  - At what point (e.g., number of consecutive "forgotten" bills or the total amount unpaid), if at all, would you do more than remind the client?
  - If you would do more, what would you do?
  - Under what circumstances, if any, would you stop seeing them because of unpaid bills?
  - Under what circumstances, if any, would you continue seeing someone who did not pay you, no matter how high the outstanding balance?
  - Would your own personal financial situation or needs at the time make any difference in your decisions?
  - What feelings do you experience as you consider these questions?
- Do you believe there are people who, under certain circumstances, can benefit from a free course of psychotherapy, or does a person need to pay at least some amount to value the therapy or for other reasons?
  - If you believe people can benefit from free treatment under certain circumstances, what are those circumstances?
  - What feelings or reactions do you have as you carefully consider these questions?
- Have you ever found it difficult to talk about your own or your family's income, wealth, difficulty making ends meet, debts, or similar financial issues?
  - What made it difficult?
  - How did you respond to the dilemma?
  - What were your feelings then, and what are your feelings about it now?

- What word or phrase best describes the meaning of money to you? Have you ever considered how the meaning you give money may affect your interactions with your clients?

- When you first decided to pursue a career in psychotherapy, what were your financial expectations and hopes?
  - Did you expect and hope to make a lot of money? Just enough to maintain a middle-class lifestyle?
  - Have your expectations and hopes changed in any way? If so, how?
  - What feelings do you experience as you consider the money you want to earn as a psychotherapist, the lifestyle you want to achieve and maintain, and similar financial issues?

- How, if at all, have your wants and need for money (for yourself, family, or special projects) influenced your choices regarding the profession you are training for or practicing?

- Have you ever asked a client what money meant to them, or if they were having a tough time paying their bills, or if they had a budget, or if they had any concerns about money? If not, why not?

Taking the time to consider and reflect on our relationship with money both personally and professionally can be one important step toward breaking the silence on this topic. It can also help us begin speaking more honestly, openly, and directly about money with our clients and colleagues.

15 TALKING ABOUT DEATH AND DYING

We are born, live, and experience inescapable encounters with death and dying. A difficult part of the human experience is the approach and arrival of the deaths of family members; friends; acquaintances; unborn children; animal companions; and, ultimately, ourselves.

And yet, even though death hovers around us—or perhaps because it does—many of us are uncomfortable with even the mention of it. We avoid the topic as if we can avoid death itself—and all of the pain, fear, uncertainty, confusion, grief, guilt, yearning, regret, and anger that come with it—by *not* talking about it.

In his landmark book, *The Denial of Death*, Becker (1973/2007) described the history of how different cultures and schools of thought created defenses to protect us from the awareness and immediacy of death, a source of terror: "This is the terror: to have emerged from nothing, to have a name, conscious-ness of self, deep inner feelings, an excruciating inner yearning for life and self-expression—and with all this yet to die" (p. 87). Samuel (2013) wrote that death was America's "greatest taboo" (para. 1). Peacock (2014) noted that the death taboo is not restricted to America; 80% of those surveyed in Britain said the Britons were uncomfortable talking about dying and death.

https://doi.org/10.1037/0000350-016
Speaking the Unspoken: Breaking the Silence, Myths, and Taboos That Hurt Therapists and Patients, by K. S. Pope, N. Y. Chavez-Dueñas, H. Y. Adames, J. L. Sonne, and B. A. Greene

Although death may be considered the final destination in some cultures, religions, and spiritual traditions, it is viewed as the beginning of a new cycle in other communities. For example, in Aztec culture, death was considered "as the beginning of a journey into a different sphere of the universe, and the entrance into another world they called the *afterlife*" (Chavez-Dueñas & Adames, in press, para. 3). The Aztecs believed that the soul or spirit of the dead lived on and it would come back to earth each year to visit their loved ones. This belief led to the annual celebration of the Day of the Dead, when Mexicans welcome back the spirits of their loved ones with food, music, and beautifully crafted altars.

The Day of the Dead tradition provides a space and time to revere, honor, and celebrate the lives of loved ones who are no longer physically present but whose memories and legacy live on. This tradition allows people who have lost the physical connection with their loved ones to maintain spiritual bonds that can transcend the boundaries of the afterlife. Like the Aztecs, the Taíno people did not view death as an end; instead, they considered death "a transitional period from one kind of existence to another" (Adames & Chavez-Dueñas, 2017, p. 25).

In many ways, death, dying, and culture are intricately connected. McCann and Adames (2013) wrote,

> Death seizes us. Death calls us. Death, as we approach the unknown, asks us to weave together strands of meaning. We move toward death, cross that ultimate threshold, simultaneously alone and together. Death is larger than us; it engulfs and overcomes us. We all die as cultural beings. Culture is the warp and the weave we use to sculpt death in a way that we can ingest, metabolize, and express. Culture forms our response to death; at times consciously, at other times simply by adoption and without question. Cultural conditions surround how we face, cry over, arrive at, court, and even conquer death. Culture and death are not separate. We narrate death and death narrates us. (p. 289)

Considering our relationship to death and the dying process and the role of culture in that process is critical in our work as therapists and clinical supervisors.

TALKING ABOUT DEATH AND DYING IN THERAPY

The topics of death and dying will almost certainly enter our therapeutic space with clients because our own personal experiences and cultures intersect with those of the people we work with (e.g., Barnett, 2009; Lantz, 1999; Marina et al., 2021; Reitsma et al., 2021; Sabucedo et al., 2020; Saracino et al., 2019). Most specifically, we are confronted with this topic when a client struggles with suicidal thoughts and impulses. Reviewing the literature, Schmitz et al. (2012) found that a majority of social workers, psychologists, psychiatrists, and trainees—in both inpatient and outpatient settings—reported that they had worked with clients with some form of suicidal thoughts or behavior. Therapists are typically well aware of our professional clinical, ethical, and legal duties to assess risk of client self-harm and to plan interventions for safeguarding the client's welfare. But that process necessarily involves talking with the client about their thoughts about, and even plans for, killing themselves. This discussion may occur repeatedly—sometimes over a period of months or more.

The topics of death and dying may arise in therapy in other ways. They may suddenly interrupt the ongoing work with a client that had been focused on a completely different issue. For example, a client's parent, partner, or child may suddenly die, or the client may receive an unexpected diagnosis of a terminal disease. Or the topic of death may be the reason an individual starts therapy. A new client may seek therapy with us to escape the aloneness they feel in their grief over the recent death of a loved one, to calm or overcome the fear they feel about their own impending death from an illness, or to explore end-of-life decisions. More recently, mental health professionals have become increasingly involved in the formal assessment of decisional competency of individuals exploring or requesting medical aid in dying, now legalized in Canada and in several states in the United States (Buote et al., 2022; S. M. Johnson et al., 2014; Werth, 1999; Werth et al., 2000). Clients look to us to help them talk about dying and death in these situations. They want and need to be heard and understood.

Most of us receive some training and supervised clinical experience in working with suicidal clients in our graduate programs and internships; in some states, that training is required for licensure (e.g., California, Kentucky, Nevada, Pennsylvania, Washington). There is a comprehensive literature on the topic as a resource for therapists (e.g., Alonzo & Gearing, 2017; Miranda & Jeglic, 2021; Robinson et al., 2022; Wasserman, 2021). More recently with our involvement in behavioral health settings, mental health graduate students are increasingly exposed to training experiences with clients facing death through their own or loved one's illness or injury. And resources for clinicians are increasingly available in the literature (e.g., Komischke-Konnerup et al., 2021; Wojtkowiak et al., 2021; Worden, 2018) and online (e.g., the American Psychological Association's, n.d., *End of Life Issues and Care* webpage).

Significant gaps, though, remain in opportunities in graduate school (and beyond) for mental health trainees and professionals to engage with a more comprehensive curriculum on death and dying, including an exploration of our own reactions to that work, of the cultural influences on those reactions, and of the impact of cultural differences between the therapist and client on discussions in therapy (Eckerd, 2009; Fang et al., 2016; Kromrey, 2021). We may feel unprepared to discuss our clients' concerns about dying and death openly, honestly, fully, and competently (see McCann & Adames, 2013). We may carry into our practice the lessons learned in our families and social groups that the topic of death is frightening, overwhelming, and best left unspoken. When therapists are avoidant, awkward, or dismissive, the processes of death and dying become even more isolating and frightening for the client, according to Elisabeth Kübler-Ross (Corr, 2019). In these situations, grieving clients suffer more (Gamino & Ritter, 2009).

Consider this poignant description of a clinical psychology graduate student's own experience with sharing (or trying to share) her grief and loss following her sister's death:

> It was the day after Thanksgiving, 2017. There was an unseasonal rain shower sprinkling Black Friday shoppers. As I drove along the highway, a delicate, light rainbow emerged from the clouds. How mystical, I thought, a winter rainbow. I pulled into my parking lot and sat in the car, finished up a podcast, and then walked into the garage to find my partner working on her car. A few moments later, I looked down at my phone and saw my dad calling. I picked up, but I think I already knew. The words came out that changed everything, "Your sister died." My legs weakened and I collapsed onto the cold concrete ground.
>
> I often replay that moment in time and find it to be just as vivid as it was three years ago. About two months later, I found myself needing support around the ton of grief now strapped to my back. Being a clinical psychology doctoral student, I reached out to student counseling services hoping to find affordable yet competent support. I filled out the intake form and got a call from the psychology intern through the college counseling center. The conversation quickly disintegrated as this (almost) psychologist tried to diagnose my grief and put me in a prescribed treatment box of group therapy. I remember telling him I was not ready for group therapy, and he responded, "Well, it's the most effective form of grief treatment." Grief treatment, what an oxymoron. Why would I want to treat my grief? Was my grief not the normal reaction for the traumatic and devastating loss of my only sister? I hung up with the intern and felt defeated and alone. I also felt disappointed by such a cold, disconnected reaction from my own supposedly empathy grounded field. (Kromrey, 2021, pp. 6–7)

How do we prepare to talk about death and dying with our clients? De Montaigne (1580/1994) suggested this: "To begin depriving death of its greatest advantage over us, let us adopt a way clean contrary to that common one; let us deprive death of its strangeness, let us frequent it, let us get used to it" (p. 24).

QUESTIONS FOR REFLECTION AND DISCUSSION

This exercise includes questions and vignettes intended to make death a little less strange to, and anxiety provoking for, each of us. Remember: Go slowly. These prompts are not intended to be completed in a one-time marathon experience.

- We begin by inviting you to engage in the 10 questions of the Dying Other, Dying Self Assessment developed by McCann and Adames (2013) and provided in Table 15.1.

- Think of a time while you were growing up when you experienced the death of a human or animal who meant a great deal to you.

  - How did your family respond to this loss?

  - Did family members share their feelings and talk about them? Do you remember how you felt—both about the death and about how your family members responded?

  - What factors in your family contributed to how they responded (e.g., culture, religion)?

  - Did anything someone said or did help you recognize, accept, and understand your feelings?

  - Did anything someone said or did make you feel worse in any way?

  - Do you think this experience has affected your current comfort with the topic of dying and death? If so, how?

TABLE 15.1. Dying Other, Dying Self Assessment

Questions for therapists to explore	Questions to explore with patients
• How do I understand death?	• What are your experiences with death?
• What does it mean to die?	• Have you ever had a loved one in palliative care before?
• What do I want for my death?	
• How does this compare or contrast to my patient's wish?	• What are your wishes for your loved one (or yourself) who is dying?
• How can I empower the patient to die in their unique manner?	• How can we bring your cultural beliefs, practices, and ceremonies into this process?
	• Who from your community can we invite into this encounter to make this happen (e.g., clergy, folk healers, artists, musicians)?

Note. Adapted from "Dying Other, Dying Self: Creating Culture and Meaning in Palliative Healthcare," by C. J. McCann and H. Y. Adames, 2013, *Palliative and Supportive Care*, 11(4), p. 292 (https://doi.org/10.1017/S1478951512000557). Copyright 2013 by Cambridge University Press. Adapted with permission.

- Take a moment and create—preferably in writing—a timeline of your own life, including the point of your imagined death (Worden & Proctor, 1976). Be as detailed as possible, particularly about the events leading up to your death. Could you share it with at least one other person? Take note of the feelings and thoughts that come up as you share.

- Imagine that you are seeing a new client for the first session. Not long after the session begins, the client tells you that their 5-year-old daughter died recently, and the client begins to cry. They then share the details of the child's tragic accidental death.

    Your client explains that the little girl was playing with her older brother out in front of their house. They were taking turns lying down on the boy's skateboard while the other pushed them along the sidewalk. With the girl on the skateboard, the boy pushed the board toward the next-door neighbor's driveway, not noticing that the neighbor was sitting in his truck parked there. Just as the girl and the board crossed the driveway, the neighbor—not seeing the girl in his rearview or side-view mirrors—backed his truck out of the driveway and ran over the child, killing her instantly.

    - As you hear your client's report, what feelings are you aware of?

    - What do you think about the girl's death? About your new client?

    - Are you reflecting on anything in your personal life as you listen?

    - Are you aware of any desire on your part to "protect" your client from their intense feelings?

    - Are you aware of any assumptions that you are making about how your client "should" be reacting to this tragic event—now or in the near future?

- Have you ever known anyone who has asked for and received help from another person to end their life, perhaps after a long illness from which they would not recover?

    - How did you feel about that?

    - Has anyone ever asked you to assist them with such a decision?

    - What factors did or would you consider in your decision whether or not to agree?

- Have you ever known anyone who requested and received medical aid in dying, or MAID, defined as the practice by which a competent adult individual with a terminal illness and deemed to have fewer than 6 months to live voluntarily self-administers a lethal dose of medication provided to them by a physician with the intention of ending their life?

- If yes, what did you think and feel about that practice?
- Have you ever had a client discuss MAID with you as a potential end-of-life choice?
- If yes, what did you think and feel?
- Has a physician ever referred a client to you to conduct a decisional competency evaluation for MAID?
- Would you ever conduct such an evaluation?
- What factors would you consider in your decision?

• You received a referral for a new client. The referral form shows that the new client is a 50-year-old immigrant woman of Latinx descent named Amalia. She presents with complicated grief following the death of her twin sister from a stroke 9 months ago. During your second session, Amalia states,

> I could not wait to come here today to share what happened. Last night, I had a conversation with my sister. She told me she loved me and asked me to let her go. I thought about it all night, and while it still hurts so much not to see her every day, I have to find a way to continue living and find joy in life while I wait to welcome her back every year during the Day of the Dead.

- What emotions are you experiencing as you listen to Amalia?
- How do you make sense of her conversation with her deceased sister?
- How would you integrate her culture and beliefs about death into your treatment plan?
- How do the client's ideologies about death and dying align or misalign with your views?

Discussing this topic in class or other group settings tends to evoke some of the most extreme differences in emotional responses to any of the other topics in this book, at least in the experience of this volume's authors. Some fall into a sad silence, volunteering at a later point that they were thinking about the recent death of a loved one or the inevitable progression of their own or a family member's disease. Others discuss research, theory, clinical techniques, and interesting facts, but in an extremely abstract way, cleared of feelings. Still, others make genuinely funny comments, seemingly releasing group tension into laughter. If we pay attention to them and greet them with respectful curiosity, these normal human responses can help us deepen our understanding of this topic and our reactions to it.

PART **IV** SPEAKING THE
UNSPOKEN–BEYOND
PSYCHOTHERAPY

16 SPEAKING UP IN SUPERVISION AND CONSULTATION

Therapy is grounded on relationships—the bond between patient and therapist. Other crucial relationships in our profession are clinical supervisor–supervisee and consultant–consultee.[1] The American Psychological Association (APA, 2014) defined *supervision* as

> a distinct professional practice employing a collaborative relationship that has both facilitative and evaluative components, that extends over time, which has the goals of enhancing the professional competence and science-informed practice of the supervisee, monitoring the quality of services provided, protecting the public, and providing a gatekeeping function for entry into the profession. (p. 9)

Falender and Shafranske (2020) defined *consultation* as

> a process of interaction between two or more professionals: the consultant, who is an expert or possesses particular competence in the area to be discussed, and the consultee, who has a particular work issue, question, or problem regarding assessment, treatment, intervention, management, organizational process, policy, or implementation of professional services. (p. 12)

---

[1]We recognize that the recipient of a consultation may be an individual, a group of individuals, or an entire organization. We use the word "consultee" to capture them all.

https://doi.org/10.1037/0000350-017
Speaking the Unspoken: Breaking the Silence, Myths, and Taboos That Hurt Therapists and Patients, by K. S. Pope, N. Y. Chavez-Dueñas, H. Y. Adames, J. L. Sonne, and B. A. Greene
Copyright © 2023 by the American Psychological Association. All rights reserved.

These professional relationships are distinct, but they share the unsurprising fact that just as there are unspoken topics in the patient–therapist relationship, various subjects also tend to be silenced in the supervisor–supervisee and the consultant–consultee dyads. The silence in supervision and consultation is multidimensional and, thus, is more complicated (A. S. Gibson et al., 2019). Unspoken topics may arise in the relationship between the therapist and their client(s), or between the supervisor with their supervisee or consultant and consultee, or in both sets of relationships (therapist–client and supervisor–supervisee/consultant–consultee; Falender & Shafranske, 2021). For example, researchers have studied nondisclosure of cultural content (e.g., cultural identity) by supervisees and their clients and reported that both types of concealment were inversely related to the supervisees' satisfaction with supervision and the supervisory working alliance (Drinane et al., 2021). This process can negatively affect clients' welfare and supervisee and consultee training. In this chapter, we focus on taboo issues in supervision and consultation.

BUILDING A LEGACY OF SPEAKING UP IN SUPERVISION AND CONSULTATION

A central goal of supervision and consultation is helping supervisees and consultees develop competency skills for delivering safe, effective, and ethical clinical services that promote patient wellness and lessen the risks of harm (Falender & Shafranske, 2020; Milne & Watkins, 2014; Pope et al., 2021; Vasquez & Johnson, 2022). The *APA Guidelines for Clinical Supervision in Health Service Psychology* (APA, 2014) and the *Guidelines for Education and Training at the Doctoral and Postdoctoral Level in Consulting Psychology (CP)/Organizational Consulting Psychology* (OCP; APA, 2017) were created to support and enhance the practices of supervision and consultation. The supervision guidelines cover seven domains: (a) supervisor competence; (b) diversity; (c) supervisory relationship; (d) professionalism; (e) assessment/ evaluation/feedback; (f) professional competence problems; and (g) ethical, legal, and regulatory considerations. The consultation guidelines present 11 competencies: (a) ethics and professional standards, (b) self-awareness and self-management, (c) relationship development, (d) diversity, (e) research methods and statistics, (f) OCP theory and case studies, (g) globalization, (h) business operations and technology, (i) assessment, (j) intervention, and (k) process consultation/action research.

These supervision and consultation guidelines are helpful, but they fail to adequately address topics silenced in the profession. How can we expect the next generation of therapists to address these topics competently and helpfully when supervisors and consultants are not provided with more specific guidance on identifying and meaningfully addressing taboo issues in supervision and consultation? If we don't talk about what has been denied, glossed over, and unspoken, we will continue the legacy of silence that many of us have inherited. We must be willing to talk about challenging, uncomfortable, or even threatening topics if we are to fulfill our professional, ethical, and clinical responsibilities to our clients, our supervisees, consultees, and the public.

As a field, we emphasize the importance of the client–therapist–supervisor triad. Over the decades, there have been more and more books, special issues, and journals dedicated to the supervision process (see Bernard & Goodyear, 2019; Borders & Brown, 2022; Callahan & Love, 2020; Falender & Shafranske, 2021). Scholar–practitioners have also turned their attention to unexamined factors that influence supervision, including environmental context (Inman & Ladany, 2014), multiculturalism (Ancis & Marshall, 2010), feminism (L. S. Brown, 2016), and racial identity development (Jernigan et al., 2010; Thrower et al., 2020):

> When supervisors are aware, open, create a space for explicit discussion of culture-specific issues, have higher racial consciousness, show vulnerability by sharing their own struggles as well as the limits of their multicultural knowledge, and focus trainees on race in case conceptualizations, it facilitates supervisee development, encourages supervisee disclosure, supports the working alliance, and ensures greater comfort in addressing cultural issues in clinical work and supervision. (Inman & Ladany, 2014, p. 644)

The supervision literature has expanded by creating models and theories that generate discussion on topics traditionally unexplored in the supervisory relationship (e.g., context, culture, race, gender). Some have proposed general recommendations for breaking the silence on a few topics in supervision (e.g., Falender & Shafranske, 2021; A. S. Gibson et al., 2019; Ladany et al., 2016). However, a noticeable gap in the supervision literature is specific guidance on how best to speak the unspoken in the client–therapist–supervisor triad.

Consultation is a relative newcomer in its recognition as a "distinct professional practice" (Falender & Shafranske, 2020, p. 11). As such, the contemporary literature exploring factors operating in the consultant–consultee relationship and, not too surprisingly, how to speak the unspoken in the client–consultee–consultant triad is lagging behind that of supervision. In the sections that follow, we offer things to consider as we work to do better.

Avoid Collusion

Our default is to collude with the silence regarding taboo topics. In supervision, *collusion* is defined as

> a joint process (conscious or unconscious) whereby both supervisor and supervisee engage in complementary safety behaviours that serve to conveniently avoid and escape from difficult topics and challenging supervision methods. Instead, they indulge in reassuring or other comforting and nonthreatening behaviours that privilege the needs of the supervisee/or over those of supervision. (Milne et al., 2009, p. 107)

Collusion further maintains the silence around taboo issues, preventing them from being addressed in supervision.

Collusion also occurs in consultation. Consider the following:

- Have you avoided a topic during supervision or consultation to protect your supervisee or consultee from feeling uncomfortable? Looking back, were you the one uneasy about the matter?

- What comes up for you when you consider openly addressing topics that your supervisee or consultee seems to be uncomfortable bringing up?

- How might you prioritize the supervisee's or consultee's needs (or your needs to have a comfortable relationship with your supervisee) instead of the client's needs?

Address the Power Differential

A power imbalance characterizes the supervisor–supervisee relationship. Although the consultant–consultee relationship is described as "nonhierarchical and collegial," the consultant is recognized as more experienced and expert (Falender & Shafranske, 2020, p. 5). Any inherent power differences in the roles of the participants are often compounded by differences in gender, race, age, immigration status, culture, ability, racial identity development, and so on. These differences can make it even more challenging to speak about silenced topics during supervision or consultation, hindering the benefit of this type of professional relationship. Recognizing the asymmetry in power is critical to developing trusting supervision and consultation relationships in which complex topics can be openly and honestly acknowledged, discussed, and addressed. The supervisor or consultant is responsible for initiating the discussion of power issues within the relationship (Grote & Heffelfinger, 2022; Porter & Vasquez, 1997).

Here are some questions to help stimulate the supervisor's or consultant's reflection on how power differences may contribute to silencing certain topics in the client–therapist–supervisor triad or the client–consultee–consultant triad:

- Are there any topics you feel particularly uncomfortable addressing in supervision or consultation?
  - If so, what are some of those topics?
  - Do the topics differ depending on whether you are the supervisor or the consultant?
- When thinking about your supervisees or consultees, how might their bringing up taboo topics in supervision or consultation impact your evaluation of them?
- What comes up as you reflect on the need to discuss taboo topics in supervision or consultation?
  - Do you worry about how supervisees or consultees may perceive you?
  - Are you concerned about the potential negative consequences of speaking up on topics often silenced in other professional settings?
  - Do you feel that you don't have enough training or confidence to discuss these issues in supervision or consultation?
- Is an open discussion about any power differential a part of your relationship building with your supervisees or consultees? If not, what are some ways to integrate this aspect into your supervision or consultation?

Model Speaking Up

Doing something we have not seen others do before can be quite challenging. Speaking up on unexplored topics in our field is difficult when we don't have role models to observe and learn from regarding how to engage professionally, candidly, and sincerely. It is easy to understand how we, as a field, find ourselves in an endless cycle of muting, hushing, and speaking around various topics rather than addressing them directly, openly, and confidently. How can we break the silence on taboo issues if we are not being planful and intentional in showing the next generation (or even our current generation) of therapists that it is okay and necessary to speak on these topics? Yes, it is difficult and it may feel awkward, and yes, we may not have the perfect words to use at the moment. However, our supervisees, consultees, and their clients deserve the best of us. Providing quality supervision and consultation requires us to address and talk about unexplored topics by modeling their importance and growth potential. It is one way to end the vicious cycle of silence

(a) between us and our supervisees and consultees and (b) between our supervisees and consultees and their clients.

Here are some questions to help you get started:

- In reflecting on your supervision and consultation, what might your supervisees or consultees learn from you about taboo topics?
- Can you recall a time when your supervisee or consultee witnessed you engage in frank and open conversations about taboo topics?
  - If so, what helped you speak up in that instance?
  - Who initiated the talk? Was it you, your supervisee, your consultee, or someone else?
  - If you cannot recall ever bringing taboo topics into supervision or consultation, what may be hindering it?
  - Are there any patterns you're noticing?
- What do we, as a profession, need to enhance our skills and confidence in role modeling open conversations about taboo topics in supervision and consultation?
- How can we purposefully model how to speak the unspoken with our supervisees and consultees?

Validate, Normalize, and Talk About the Awkwardness

Talking about unspoken topics can evoke various emotions, including discomfort and awkwardness. The lack of experience or practice in how to openly talk about unspoken subjects may contribute to our feeling insecure and incompetent. We may wonder how best to begin the conversation, what words to use, and how to manage the discomfort. It is expected that we will feel awkward talking about topics we have not discussed before in professional settings. If we are being honest, we may not even have these conversations in our personal lives. The best way to deal with these emotions is simply acknowledging to ourselves that they exist. We can begin by validating that it is difficult, and, yes, it may feel weird or uncomfortable, but these thorny topics are critical to discuss for the advancement of the field and the betterment of ourselves, our clients, supervisees, and consultees.

Here are some questions that may be helpful to start the conversation:

- What may be creating feelings of awkwardness?
  - Is it a lack of experience and practice?
  - Could it be fear of how you may be perceived?
  - Or a gap of knowledge on the topic?

- How does your culture express and address emotions?
  - Are they expressed and spoken about openly or hushed and suppressed?
  - How has your culture impacted how you address and express emotions?

- How has your own training and experience with supervision, consultation, or both, influenced how you deal with feelings of awkwardness? How has this shaped you in your supervisory style?

- How does awkwardness, discomfort, or other feelings show up nonverbally?

QUESTIONS FOR REFLECTION AND DISCUSSION

In this section, we provide several questions and scenarios to stimulate discussion on speaking the unspoken in supervision and consultation. We encourage you to engage in the exercises with one or more people.

Exercise: Looking at Our Own History as a Supervisee or Consultee

Each of us has our own history in the role of supervisees or consultees. Some of us can remember working with supervisors or consultants who were warm, caring, and, at the same time, honest and direct. Others may have encountered supervisors or consultants who were distant, uncaring, or even hostile.

As you reflect on your overall history as a supervisee and consultee, consider the following questions.

- How trusting and secure did you feel in your relationships with people who have supervised you throughout your career or provided consulting services to you or your place of employment?

- What, if anything, made you feel nervous, uncomfortable, irritated, disappointed, apprehensive, angry, or frustrated?

- How comfortable were you talking about mistakes you made during therapy sessions; difficulties understanding or helping the client; ideas inconsistent with the supervisor's or consultant's theoretical orientation; sexual feelings; issues of race, culture, sexual/affectional orientation, religion; and so on?

- Did you keep any secrets from your supervisor?

- Were you ever attracted to a client? If so, did you tell your supervisor or consultant?

- Were you ever attracted to your supervisor or consultant? If so, did you tell them?

Exercise: Looking at Our Reactions to Various Scenarios Involving a Supervisee or Consultee

Now that you have reflected on your personal history as a supervisee and consultee, we invite you to consider and think through a few scenarios.

Scenario 1

One of your supervisees works with an 18-year-old college student who is 8 weeks pregnant. While watching a recording of one of their sessions, the client discusses "not being ready to become a mother." The client states, "I am conflicted about whether to have an abortion; it just goes against my religious beliefs. If my parents found out, they would disown me." As you continue watching the therapy session, the client proceeds to explain that she needs to decide soon because her ob-gyn tells her that the longer she waits, the more difficult it will be for her to find access to abortion health services in her state.

• What are your emotional reactions as you envision yourself watching the therapy session?

• What are some thorny themes that come up for you in this scenario? Are any of the themes difficult for you to address?

• Which aspect(s) of the scenario (ob-gyn, parents, client, religion) do you feel more connected to? Why? How might this impact how you decide to proceed in supervision?

• What course of supervisory actions are you considering?

Scenario 2

You begin to smell something awful in the middle of a consultation meeting. You get up from your chair, look in the trash, and see that the bin is empty— nothing there. You ask if your consultee smells it. The consultee says they do not. You look under your shoes to see if you've stepped on something, ask the consultee to do the same, and again, nothing. When consultation ends, you open the door to escape the smell without success. As you walk (and sniff) around the room, you notice that the chair where your consultee was sitting is infused with a foul odor. The smell returns in the following consultation session, confirming that it comes from your consultee.

• Imagine yourself in this scenario. What are some thoughts and emotional reactions you're having?

• Have you experienced something similar in the past? If so, how did you address it?

- What factors that affect odor variations among people would need to be considered in this case?

- What are some ways in which the consultee's odor may be impacting their work with clients? What about their work with you?

- How would you handle this situation in a thoughtful and respectful but direct way?

- Turning the tables, how do you envision yourself responding if the consultee respectfully shares that they're experiencing a body odor coming from you?

Scenario 3

You are a supervisor at a practicum site for first-year, master's-level students who provide mental health services at a local outpatient clinic. Once a week, you go to the clinic to do supervision. You have become familiar with your supervisees' affect and emerging therapeutic styles.

On this particular occasion, as you're watching from behind the two-way mirror, you notice one of your supervisees gleefully smiling at their client. Their tone of voice and nonverbals with this client are different; the session has a quality best described as flirtatious. The supervisee's reaction is atypical because they usually have a more serious demeanor in their sessions with clients.

- What are your emotional reactions as you envision yourself behind the two-way mirror?

- Have you unintentionally engaged in flirtation behaviors or fantasies about a client?
  - If so, how did you navigate that situation?
  - Did you bring it up to your supervisor or consult with a peer?
  - If not, what barriers prevented you from discussing it in supervision or seeking consultation?
  - If you found yourself in this situation again, what would you do differently?
  - Would you consider sharing this experience with the client? Why or why not?

- What are some thorny themes that come up for you in this scenario? Are any of the themes difficult for you to address?

- What course of supervisory actions are you considering?

- What gender did you envision for the client and your supervisee?
  - Would you respond any differently if the client and supervisee were of the same gender?
  - What if both the client and supervisee were the same or different gender as you?
  - What if the supervisee were of the same or different sexual/affectional orientation as you?
- Considering the client–therapist–supervisor triad in the context of this scenario, have you been attracted to your supervisee?
  - If so, how did you navigate that situation?
  - Did you bring it up to your supervisor or consult with a peer?
  - If not, what barriers prevented you from talking about it in supervision or seeking consultation?
  - If you found yourself in this situation again, what would you do differently?

In closing, addressing taboo topics in supervision and consultation is not easy, but it is essential. As supervisors and consultants, we are responsible for training and guiding practitioners while ensuring quality and ethical care to our supervisee's or consultee's clients. We believe supervision and consultation are other pathways to help unmute the cycle of silence within the profession.

17 SPEAKING UP IN THE PROFESSION AND THE COMMUNITY

Speaking up is hard for most of us, a paradox for the talking profession and a common theme throughout this book. As therapists, we are trained to work with clients and communities, conduct research, work in organizations, mentor and supervise students, and engage in public speaking. Yet, when it comes to taboo topics, we are often at a loss of words, or we may not recognize the need to speak up. When we decide to discuss silenced subjects, we may feel anxious, unsure, or afraid. Each of the five authors of this volume has had that experience—more than once. We may wonder if it is better to just keep quiet. Or to speak secretly with only one or two trusted friends. It can be hard to find the strength, courage, and resolution to talk openly, candidly, and directly about these challenging topics, to say what we truly believe and what is in our hearts.

We hope that, by now, you're appreciating the challenge of breaking the silence about taboo topics and how speaking up is critical to our work as therapists. This chapter moves our focus from psychotherapy, supervision, and consultation to speaking up in the profession (e.g., professional associations) and the local community to which we belong. Speaking up in the profession is crucial because it has the power to create and enforce rules,

https://doi.org/10.1037/0000350-018
Speaking the Unspoken: Breaking the Silence, Myths, and Taboos That Hurt Therapists and Patients, by K. S. Pope, N. Y. Chavez-Dueñas, H. Y. Adames, J. L. Sonne, and B. A. Greene

regulations, and standards that guide professional conduct and practice, which directly impact treatment and patient care. If speaking with clients about taboo topics is difficult, talking about these areas in the profession may be even more complex. We may fear being shunned by our colleagues, seen as troublemakers, laughed at, criticized as "not a team player," or dismissed altogether within professional circles. And, of course, colleagues may stop referring new clients to us or close the doors to other professional opportunities.

We invite you to explore the following questions with colleagues, students, and supervisees:

- Is speaking up in the profession a personal choice?

- What if remaining silent can cause harm to the clients and communities we serve in our roles as therapists, supervisors, or consultants? Can you think of examples of how the harm might occur?

- What message do we send by not talking about taboo topics? What are we saying with our silence?

In the following sections, we provide ways to help us think through the nuances and unique challenges of talking about difficult topics in the field and with community members.

DELIBERATELY SPEAKING THE UNSPOKEN IN THE PROFESSION

Speaking up in the profession can create important discussions, play a vital role in our own and others' personal and professional growth, and help bring about positive change in the field. In this section, we provide key actions to better equip us to speak frankly about difficult topics.

Be on the Lookout for Taboo Topics in the Profession

Developing an awareness of silenced topics in the field is a prerequisite to speaking up. Part III of this volume provided examples and questions for discussion and reflection to help us practice talking while gaining hands-on experience in how challenging it is to talk openly and honestly about unspoken topics. However, this list of topics is not exhaustive, and shifting our focus from therapy to the profession and community adds to the already demanding process. Consider the following:

- What topics would you add to those presented in Chapters 7 through 15?
- What clues, cues, or patterns can we look for to help identify when a topic is being silenced in the profession?

- How can we continue to increase our awareness about what we are collectively not paying attention to and talking about in the field?

Prepare Yourself

Talking about topics that often are not discussed openly, sincerely, and directly in the profession requires thoughtful planning. We need to consider the best possible way to bring up a subject so others can become curious and join in the dialogue. We also need to consider our goals and methods and the best language to use to start and support discussion and action with our colleagues. And we need to keep in mind the role of social power in the exchange and the power of an individual or small group of people to bring about change.

Identify Goals

Reflecting on the reason(s) why we have chosen to speak up can help us determine how best to proceed. Consider the following:

- What are you seeking to accomplish by speaking up on a particular topic?

- Is your intent to bring attention to the topic in the field?

- Or are you speaking about an issue and expecting or working toward a specific outcome (e.g., position statement, professional guidelines, revision of existing standards, practices, and mission statements, public service campaign, increased funding)?

Know Your Audience and Consider Social Power Dynamics

An essential part of speaking up successfully is considering who the listeners are. Knowing our intended audience can help shape our message, determine how best to deliver it, anticipate how the content may be received, and create a Plan B if we meet resistance. Although these factors are essential, they're not enough. We need to also consider how social power may support, undermine, or complicate our efforts in the current situation. Using race as an example, Helms (1990) developed the social interaction model to describe how social power influences whether exchanges between and among people are experienced as (a) growth promoting, (b) contentious, (c) conflictual, or (d) stagnant (see also Adames et al., in press; Helms, 2019; Jernigan et al., 2010; Thrower et al., 2020).

Keeping the social interaction model (Helms, 1990) in mind can help us navigate and decide how best to approach our audience to create growth-promoting exchanges. Even in cases in which you are speaking with colleagues, imbalances in social power may be present because of race, gender, age, and other social group identities. Power imbalance may also be heightened when the audience comprises people who hold positions of power (e.g., supervisors, administrators, presidents of professional associations) compared with those with less power in the profession (e.g., supervisees, students, junior scholars, nonboard members of a professional association).

We encourage you to engage the following questions, which we've found helpful in preparing to speak up:

- What are some ways to carefully consider the implications of speaking and not speaking up to these audiences?

- Is there anything that we should avoid doing or saying when considering the power imbalance?

- How do we deliver a message that takes power imbalance into account and increases the likelihood of producing the desired outcome?

- In cases in which we may have less power relative to our audience, what price are we willing to pay to create positive change?

- What "buttons" are you willing to push?

- How would you manage when your "buttons" are the ones that are being pushed?

- What motivates you to speak up publicly?

  - Is it the ethical values and principles of the profession?

  - Respect for human rights?

  - Your own personal values?

  - Other motivators?

Pick a Method

Next, consider effective processes to engage our audience's curiosity and help achieve our goal. For instance, if our goal is to raise awareness on an issue that has been historically and currently silenced in the profession, what professional platforms are available to you for engaging colleagues in an open discussion? Possibilities include informal roundtable discussions, a symposium at conference, organizing a special issue in a journal, and social media events to generate activity surrounding the topic. We need to support our message, argument, and advocacy with evidence and ethical persuasion.

Consider these questions:

- What is the evidence (e.g., clinical observations, research studies, narratives) and ethical reasons for importance of this topic and your responsibility to speak up?

- Which platforms make you most comfortable while discussing uncomfortable topics?

- What process would increase the chance of helping break the silence on the topic?

- Who in your professional circles do you trust to invite to join you in these efforts?

Take Action and Debrief

Our field provides us with a variety of venues to speak the unspoken. A major outlet is publishing, including books, chapters, newsletters, journal articles, special issues, and commentaries on published scholarship. Other outlets include traditional presentations at conferences and conventions, including symposia and webinars, and less-traditional ones, such as podcasts, Instagram Live, and other social media spaces. These and other outlets are spaces to speak about the unspoken in the profession. They also provide ways of modeling to peers, colleagues, and students how to name, discuss, engage, navigate, and dismantle systems that silence taboo topics in the field. In the end, whichever outlet you choose, we encourage debriefing afterward with yourself and others.

To help stimulate reflections and discussion, consider the following:

- What did you learn from speaking up in the profession?

- Was the experience as scary, uncomfortable, or fulfilling—or all three— as you envisioned it?

- What worked? What didn't work?

- Do you wish you had known something (or some things) you now know?

- In what ways is speaking up in the profession similar to and different from speaking up in a small group? What about in comparison with speaking with a client, student, supervisee, colleague, or peer?

- How, if at all, did speaking up in this particular forum affect your framing of the silenced topic?

- If our goal of speaking up did not have the intended outcome on the first try, how do we move forward and try again?

SPEAKING UP IN THE COMMUNITY

Talking about difficult issues in the community (e.g., oppression, White supremacy culture, abortion, guns, politics, death and dying) with the people most affected by them is crucial for putting advocacy into practice and helping create a sustainable, life-affirming, and humane society. Speaking up in the community about difficult topics brings unique challenges beyond those already outlined regarding initiating such discussions. For example, we may be particularly aware of our professional responsibility to present ourselves as competent representatives of our field in the community. We may not be immediately aware of, or feel comfortable with, the particular culture of the community or how to balance our relative social power as professionals. We may also experience concerns for our personal safety as we enter community discussions about controversial topics.

The action plan described earlier—remaining alert to taboo topics, identifying goals, considering social power, knowing your audience, picking a method, and taking action and debriefing—can help us toward that goal. As members of the profession, how may we contribute or collude, either with our action or inaction, to the silencing of certain topics in the community? Considering the following questions may help us answer that question:

- How can we engage and learn from community members how to best speak up on taboo topics while maintaining cultural humility?

- What can we do to ensure that we, as the professionals, are not the only ones doing the talking?

- How can we better listen to what members of the community have to say?

- How can we ensure we take cultural differences and unique community customs into account when choosing a delivery method?

- What are effective mediums to communicate about taboo topics with the community? Some ways to translate psychological knowledge include

  - creating tool kits, infographics, blogs, op-ed pieces;

  - doing media appearances on local television and radio stations to discuss silenced topics; or

  - engaging in public speaking in community settings like public webinars, community roundtable discussions, listening sessions, and town hall forums.

- Which public forum do you feel the most comfortable in engaging the community?

- Would you feel more at ease if you had a colleague join you in this endeavor?

- Is what you have to say within your professional scope of practice?

In closing, one way to end the silence that hurts people and society is by speaking up. Sometimes we break the silence by taking the courageous actions to talk with people in our field. Other times, we disturb the silence by engaging the community. And, yes, we can also stop the silence by speaking to ourselves.

What matters is that we consistently engage in acts of speaking up about issues that we and others have avoided, shrouded in myth, blurred through abstractions and jargon, and silenced. We can think of no better way to end this chapter than with the words of Martin Luther King, Jr. (n.d.): "Our lives begin to end the day we become silent about things that matter" (para. 1).

PART V BUT WHAT IF . . .

18

HITTING A WALL, OR THE WALL HITTING US

What to Do When Confused, Scared, Disheartened, or Stuck

You've worked hard to get this far in exploring unspoken topics. You've faced the challenge of looking inward to identify and explore issues that we've learned to avoid. You've listened for clues about what is not being said by examining external systems that create and sustain the silence. And you've recognized how we can knowingly or unintentionally sabotage the process of breaking the silence.

There will be times, however, when we confront an unspoken topic and don't know what to do. Part of the nature of these topics is that they are not often talked about openly, honestly, and directly in training programs, collegial discussions, or much of anywhere. It makes sense, then, that we haven't received much guidance on what to do. And, even a temporary "not knowing what to do" can freeze us into a paralyzing impasse in our work with a patient. Feeling frozen can touch off alarm bells coupled with the discomfort already inherent in a taboo topic. We may ask ourselves whether we are even competent to practice or if, perhaps, we are not smart enough, not well-trained enough, or not emotionally solid enough. We may fear that others (including our patients) will recognize our incompetence. We may feel that our supervisors will judge

https://doi.org/10.1037/0000350-019
Speaking the Unspoken: Breaking the Silence, Myths, and Taboos That Hurt Therapists and Patients, by K. S. Pope, N. Y. Chavez-Dueñas, H. Y. Adames, J. L. Sonne, and B. A. Greene

us negatively, that we'll be thrown out of grad school or fired from our jobs, or our patients may quit therapy, and referrals will stop. Or, that "not knowing what to do" can trigger a quick reaction just to rid ourselves of the burden of not knowing. That immediate reaction may not be therapeutic—or worse, it may be harmful to the patient and the therapeutic relationship. Then, other alarm bells sound. We worry about the patient's welfare, getting sued, or having our license revoked. Before long, all we can hear are those alarm bells without a solution in sight.

So, what do we do when we don't know what to do? We recommend asking ourselves questions frequently during the course of therapy, particularly when treatment seems stuck. Is there an unspoken issue here that may be interfering with or blocking the therapeutic process with the patient? If so, what is it? What does it mean? How are we, as therapists contributing to the impasse? How is the patient contributing? What are some options for how to respond? What are the likely effects of each option?

In this chapter, we offer suggestions that may be helpful with this line of questioning. There's nothing special about these suggestions. They tend to be routinely discussed in our training and our practices. But alarm bells can interfere with our ability to remember and put them to use when we need them most. We want to repeat another theme of this book here: There is no one-size-fits-all way to approach unspoken topics or to understand their nature and implications for therapy. And, we want to stress that there is no one way of responding, either. Various theoretical orientations offer different, sometimes opposing, ways of approaching such quandaries. Each therapist, patient, therapeutic relationship, and situation is different. An approach that's helpful in one instance can head us in the wrong direction in another.

RESIST A KNEE-JERK REACTION

Not knowing what to do in a therapy session when an unspoken topic arises can make us uncomfortable. We are left to sit in silence for a moment—or longer—when seconds can feel like hours, burdened with the emotional distress triggered by the topic and the tension created as we struggle to understand what is going on and figure out what to do next. All with the patient looking at us expectantly. There is often a mighty temptation to immediately lift that burden by saying anything, even if it's not on point. Reacting to stop the discomfort risks interrupting the mutual exploration with our clients, stopping a therapeutic process, and interfering with, or even rupturing, a trusting alliance.

An alternative to reacting in a knee-jerk way is training ourselves to be okay with doing nothing for a while until we can catch our breath and connect our gut feelings with our brains. We can then reflect and formulate the questions that help us define the taboo topic, contemplate its meaning, and consider how to respond. Choosing not to react immediately may sound like an invitation to collude with the silencing of the topic. It is not. The silence here is in the service of understanding the patient, the unspoken topic, and the most therapeutic response. This recommendation may also feel like a threat to our intuition, spontaneity, and creativity. It doesn't need to be. This step allows therapists time to let our intuitions and creativity unfold with less constriction from negative feelings of anxiety, confusion, fear, or anger, lending perhaps to even greater spontaneity.

ASSESS AND, IF NECESSARY AND POSSIBLE, STRENGTHEN COMPETENCE

Is it possible that we feel stuck and at a loss for what to do next when an unspoken topic arises because of our lack of competence—a lack of knowledge or skills? The initial sessions with the client may have stayed within areas of our specialization or even expertise. But, somehow, the client's situation may have moved, perhaps gradually and subtly, into areas for which we've had virtually no education, training, or supervised experience—not surprising if the topic is taboo. Or perhaps, as therapy progresses, a client may trust us with topics and areas of their lives they had previously hesitated to disclose. A careful assessment of the client's current psychological status, pressing issues, evolution of the treatment plan, and our competencies in those areas may help to answer that question. If the answer is yes, we've slid into a place of incompetence. The next question is whether additional education (e.g., reading relevant studies and other literature, attending continuing education workshops), supervision, or consultation can quickly enhance our competence to help us know what to do without compromising the client's welfare.

Theory, research, practices, professional guidelines, and standards of care constantly evolve regardless of our specialty areas, the populations we serve, and the interventions we use. When stuck, it is almost always worth conducting a literature search or using some other means to find out whether there are new theoretical contributions, research findings, practice innovations, guidelines and "best practices," or other information and resources that could clarify how we arrived at an impasse and how to move forward with this client in this situation.

The internet is a rich resource for finding helpful literature, especially for those without convenient access to an academic or professional library. PsycInfo, Medline, and various other databases have abstracts of theoretical, research, practice, and review articles. In addition, information from other mental health professionals (e.g., in blogs or free, continuing education PowerPoint presentations) is often accessible by searching for a topic on the internet.

In many cases, we have the time and resources available to bring our competence up to speed for a particular client. But sometimes, achieving competence for a specific situation will not be possible. In such cases, it is crucial that we be honest with ourselves about the limits of our competence and our clinical, ethical, and legal responsibilities when we lack adequate competence. We need to consider possibilities for helping the client to find someone competent to work with them on their specific problems.

Our recommendation to seek supervision or consultation presents a seeming contradiction. How can we suggest talking to someone about something we don't usually talk about and we don't know how to talk about? We recommend this because our reluctance to disclose to others an uncomfortable topic that has emerged with a client, or a potential course of action in response, is a red flag that we've stumbled across an unspoken topic that we need to understand. Find a trusted colleague, supervisor, or consultant, and start talking. Start asking questions.

Using supervision or consultation to learn more about and gain competence for a taboo topic is likely easier if we already have established this resource as a regular part of our clinical activities. For those of us already licensed and out in practice, forming a network of trusted colleagues and clinical mentors with whom we can talk out issues can help us make sure that our work does not fall into needless errors, unintentional malpractice, or harmful actions because of lack of knowledge, guidance, perspective, challenge, or support in general and particularly around unspoken topics. Therapists-in-training are often assigned supervisors and may not feel they have much freedom to seek out individuals with different perspectives. We encourage trainees to talk first with their assigned supervisors, even if they must open up a discussion of the taboo topic. When necessary, include the suggestion that both the supervisor and supervisee seek consultation from a third party (See Chapter 16 for a discussion of supervision and consultation regarding unspoken topics.)

Regardless of whether our supervision or consultation happens on a regular basis or on an as-needed basis, our methods for choosing individuals with whom to talk about difficult topics can affect the integrity of the process. Including colleagues, clinical mentors, and supervisors with different theoretical orientations, training experiences, areas of clinical expertise, and social group identities, although potentially challenging at times, is crucial in our exploration and discovery. We close off new learning and risk only superficial or pro forma results if we choose only supervisors and consultants who'll reflect our own thinking rather than show us new ways of approaching a problem.

REVIEW THE CHART AND THE CASE

Reviewing the client's chart and the situation can suggest a way out of our impasse or reveal factors that contributed to our not knowing what to do. As you look at the chart now, does it reflect accurately and realistically what you know about the client? Are there omissions or significant pieces of information that appear minimized, distorted, or just plain wrong now that you have more history with the patient? Were any aspects of the referral questions, the client's initial statement of the problem (i.e., the reason for seeking professional help), assessment, or treatment plan not followed up on? Were there any themes that seemed to stop abruptly, any matters you had intended to explore further or later that still have not been clarified or addressed? What have been the outcomes of various interventions with the client? If any have been not so positive, why do you think that happened? How would you describe your therapeutic alliance and other aspects of your relationship with the client?

The chart review and your thoughts about the paralyzing unspoken topic(s) operating in the therapy can help generate ideas about how to proceed on our own or with consultation or supervision. As you do so, consider how you might document your interventions. Is there any hesitance to completely and accurately chart what you plan to do, and why? Imagine the potential outcomes of your plan, including the worst-case scenario in which everything goes wrong. The results of this exercise can help you know more about what you might do and choose among your options for moving through or past your impasse.

LOOK FOR LOGICAL FLAWS

We may seem to have all of the information we need about the client, the client's history, current condition, and the relevant theory and research, yet we're still caught in an impasse of not knowing what to do. It may not be the information and ideas that are the problem but how we're putting them together. Are we making mistakes in logic that are leading us astray? It may be helpful to review some common logical fallacies to determine whether any plays a role in creating the impasse. Here are a few that seem most relevant. You may think of others.

Slippery Slope

The slippery slope logical flaw asserts that a specific course of action will inevitably lead to a series of future events. The line of reasoning starts with a relatively benign fact but leads to an unlikely or even ridiculous negative outcome with no supporting evidence.

> *Example*: "My client just told me they forgot their checkbook and cannot pay me at the end of our session. They said they would mail me a check as soon as they got home. But they'll forget, and past behavior being the best predictor of future behavior, they'll run up a huge bill of unpaid sessions. I'm barely getting by as it is. I'm going to miss my office rent payments, get evicted, and have to close my practice. I'm going to go bankrupt."

Hasty Generalization

A hasty generalization is a conclusion based on a few experiences rather than substantial proof.

> *Example*: "Two of my clients recently terminated therapy after the first few sessions. Both of them expressed their fears of death. One was concerned about a recent cancer diagnosis, and the other worried about chronic heart disease. Therefore, any discussions of death with clients should be avoided."

Affirming the Consequent

This fallacy takes the form of:

$$\text{If } X, \text{ then } Y.$$

$$Y.$$

$$\text{Therefore, } X.$$

> *Example*: "Therapists who ultimately become inappropriately sexually involved with a patient often start by discussing the patient's sexual concerns. My patient and I are talking about my patient's sexuality. I'm going to end up having sex with my patient."

False Dilemma

Also known as the *either–or* fallacy of *false choices,* this logical error only acknowledges two (one of which is usually extreme) options from an array of possibilities.

> *Example*: "Either I immediately address the issue that my patient has made several critical comments about others with my sexual orientation, or I have to terminate our therapy relationship."

IDENTIFY ANY UNUSUAL BEHAVIORS

In addition to reviewing common logical fallacies to determine if they are playing a role in creating the impasse in therapy, it may be helpful to spend some time reflecting on your past session(s) with your client. Have you been acting in any way or considering acting in some way that is outside of your usual behaviors in therapy? There is, of course, no suggestion here that unusual behaviors (or thoughts of unusual behaviors) are, per se, signs of something wrong. Most therapists likely stray from usual procedures and engage in creative interventions from time to time. But actions that appear considerably different from our general practice probably warrant special notice and consideration. They may provide important clues to understanding and dealing with that uneasy feeling of not knowing what to do as the therapeutic work stalls.

It may be that some unusual behaviors reflect our own avoidance of an unspoken topic beyond our immediate awareness that has emerged in our work with a client. For example, you might notice that you tend to interrupt a particular client more often than others or interrupt one client repeatedly during discussions on a particular topic. You might become aware that you have "forgotten" an appointment with one patient more than once. You might realize you get so sleepy with a client that you can barely resist dozing off. You might call a client by the wrong name. Or you might find that you repeatedly imagine standing up and embracing your client as you listen to them talk. When we take the time to review our work and examine the context of these unusual behaviors, we may be able to identify the topic. We might realize that they tend to occur when we sense the client's or our own anger or sexuality, or fear. Once we can pinpoint the topic, our options about how to respond will likely become clearer, and the chances of moving beyond the impasse will increase.

It may also be that some unusual behaviors are quite intentional and direct responses to a taboo area that has emerged in an all-too-obvious way to us, setting off strong internal distress alarms. For example, we may have yelled at or sworn at a client who was expressing intense anger toward us. Or we might have moved our chair from its usual position to one farther away from a client with a physical difference. We may realize that we have started our past several sessions just a bit late for a client we are frustrated with over unpaid fees or who talks session after session about the death of their beloved pet. Examining the context of these atypical behaviors can provide what we need to know to start figuring out what to do.

REFRESH FAMILIARITY WITH ETHICAL PRINCIPLES, STANDARDS, AND LAWS

When caught in an impasse, it can be helpful to make sure that we're up to date with the most current ethical principles, professional standards, legislation, and case law relevant to our practice. Professional organizations (e.g., American Psychological Association, National Association of Social Workers, American Association of Marriage and Family Therapy, Canadian Psychological Association) update and revise ethics codes often in response to complex contemporary dilemmas encountered by working members (e.g., regarding therapist involvement in multiple nonsexual relationships with clients, innovative technologies, emergency situations). In the same way, legislators and judges change state and federal mental health laws. Reviewing the professional, ethical, and legal standards that govern our work can provide unexpected perspectives and insights.

It may be that the impasse is complicated by a not-so-uncommon conflict between a therapist's values and professional principles or the law, or between two professional ethical principles or standards, or between a professional ethics code and the law. For example, a therapist may hold compassion for other humans as a deep personal conviction and may wonder what the right course is when a long-term patient pleads with them to keep confidential the fact that, in a moment of exhaustion and frustration, the patient hit their 2-year-old child in the face, causing a bruise. Or a therapist may think that a patient with severe anorexia needs to be hospitalized for their welfare. Still, the patient has worked hard in therapy to develop their independence and a sense of autonomy, and they vehemently refuse to be admitted. Or a therapist may be asked to see a very angry preadolescent child in therapy by the child's parents, who give their legal consent to treatment, but the child refuses—talk about paralyzing situations.

In these circumstances, it is helpful to have a decision-making model that defines specific, concrete steps you can take as you reason and feel your way through the impasse. Sonne and Weniger (2018) proposed a decision-making process that integrates many elements absent from previous models. Drawing on diverse ethical, cultural, and theoretical perspectives, Pope et al. (2021) discussed 17 practical steps for understanding, thinking through, and responding effectively to ethical dilemmas, especially when we face conflicting values and ethical gray zones. The steps propose a process to help identify key facts and aspects of a situation, consider the benefits and drawbacks of our options, and discover or create better approaches.

KEEP QUESTIONING

One of the most valuable—likely necessary—suggestions when caught in an impasse is to continue the process of questioning. Even after we have some answers, persistent questioning can be viewed as a fundamentally important aspect of psychological science and practice (Pope, 1997). The recommendations outlined earlier might be characterized as aids in creating and developing our questions about what we don't know. What new advances in theory, research, or practice do we not know that a literature search might uncover? What information about the patient have we overlooked? What logical errors might have crept into our attempts to piece together our information? What could a consultant tell us? An even more important question is, Why do I resist asking questions like the ones in this chapter?

We can also revisit earlier chapters in this book. It may be helpful to review the self-assessment in Chapter 5 or exercises in Chapters 7 through 15 a second, third, or fourth time with a particular client in mind. We may observe a new or different emotional reaction or insight that provides an understanding of an impasse and a direction for the therapy.

Throughout this process, but particularly if the impasse persists, the questioning might also take another direction: toward what we know—or at least what we think we know. The continued exploration and questioning of our most honored values, cherished beliefs, long-standing assumptions, basic practices, and professional ethical and legal standards, no matter how dear, prestigious, or popular the source, can sometimes lead us to the most unexpected discoveries and meaningful progress with patients.

It is worth reminding ourselves of this critical aspect of our identity as psychological scientists and practitioners. Whatever answers we have—or think we have—at one moment in time, we are never without questions and a willingness to pursue them wherever they lead.

References

Adames, H. Y., & Chavez-Dueñas, N. Y. (2017). *Cultural foundations and interventions in Latino/a mental health: History, theory, and within-group differences*. Routledge Press. https://doi.org/10.4324/9781315724058

Adames, H. Y., & Chavez-Dueñas, N. Y. (2021). Reclaiming all of me: The Racial Queer Identity Framework. In K. L. Nadal & M. Scharron del Rio (Eds.), *Queer psychology: Intersectional perspectives* (pp. 59–79). Springer. https://doi.org/10.1007/978-3-030-74146-4_4

Adames, H. Y., Chavez-Dueñas, N. Y., & Jernigan, M. M. (2021). The fallacy of a raceless Latinidad: Action guidelines for centering Blackness in Latinx psychology. *Journal of Latina/o Psychology, 9*(1), 26–44. https://doi.org/10.1037/lat0000179

Adames, H. Y., Chavez-Dueñas, N. Y., & Jernigan, M. M. (in press). Dr. Janet E. Helms: Envisioning and creating a more humane psychological science, theory, and practice. *American Psychologist*. Advance online publication. https://doi.org/10.1037/amp0001037

Adames, H. Y., Chavez-Dueñas, N. Y., Lewis, J. A., Neville, H. A., French, B. H., Chen, G. A., & Mosley, D. V. (2022). Radical healing in psychotherapy: Addressing the wounds of racism-related stress and trauma. *Psychotherapy*. Advance online publication. https://doi.org/10.1037/pst0000435

Adames, H. Y., Chavez-Dueñas, N. Y., Sharma, S., & La Roche, M. J. (2018). Intersectionality in psychotherapy: The experiences of an AfroLatinx queer immigrant. *Psychotherapy, 55*(1), 73–79. https://doi.org/10.1037/pst0000152

Adames, H. Y., Chavez-Dueñas, N. Y., Vasquez, M. J. T., & Pope, K. S. (2023). *Succeeding as a therapist: How to create a thriving practice in a changing world*. American Psychological Association. https://doi.org/10.1037/0000321-000

Adams, M., Blumenfeld, W. J., Catalano, D. C. J., Dejong, K., Hackman, H. W., Hopkins, L. E., Love, B., Peters, M. L., Shlasko, D., & Zúñiga, X. (2018). *Readings for diversity and social justice* (4th ed.). Routledge.

Agathangelou, A. M., & Ling, L. H. M. (2002). An unten(ur)able position: The politics of teaching for women of color in the US. *International Feminist Journal of Politics, 4*(3), 368–398. https://doi.org/10.1080/1461674022000031562

Ahn, L. H., Yee, S. E., Dixon, K. M., Kase, C. A., Sharma, R., & Hill, C. E. (2020). Feeling offended by clients: The experiences of doctoral student therapists. *Journal of Counseling Psychology.* Advance online publication. https://doi.org/10.1037/cou0000511

Alonzo, D., & Gearing, R. E. (2017). *Suicide assessment and treatment: Empirical and evidence-based practices* (2nd ed.). Springer Publishing Company. https://doi.org/10.1891/9780826135155

Alpert, J. L., Steinberg, A., & Courtois, C. A. (2021). Epilogue: Prevention and intervention. In A. Steinberg, J. L. Alpert, & C. A. Courtois (Eds.), *Sexual boundary violations in psychotherapy: Facing therapist indiscretions, transgressions, and misconduct* (pp. 385–407). American Psychological Association. https://doi.org/10.1037/0000247-021

Alvarez, A. N., Liang, C. T. H., & Neville, H. A. (Eds.). (2016). *The cost of racism for People of Color: Contextualizing experiences of discrimination.* American Psychological Association. https://doi.org/10.1037/14852-000

American Civil Liberties Union. (2022). *Nationwide anti-mosque activity.* ACLU. https://www.aclu.org/issues/national-security/discriminatory-profiling/nationwide-anti-mosque-activity

American Psychological Association. (n.d.). *End of life issues and care.* https://www.apa.org/pi/aging/programs/eol

American Psychological Association. (2007). *Responding therapeutically to patient expression of sexual attraction: A stimulus training tape* [Videocassette].

American Psychological Association. (2012a). Guidelines for assessment of and intervention with persons with disabilities. *American Psychologist, 67*(1), 43–62. https://doi.org/10.1037/a0025892

American Psychological Association. (2012b). Guidelines for psychological practice with lesbian, gay, and bisexual clients. *American Psychologist, 67*(1), 10–42. https://doi.org/10.1037/a0024659

American Psychological Association. (2014). *APA guidelines for clinical supervision in health service psychology.* https://www.apa.org/about/policy/guidelines-supervision.pdf

American Psychological Association. (2015). Guidelines for psychological practice with transgender and gender nonconforming people. *American Psychologist, 70*(9), 832–864. https://doi.org/10.1037/a0039906

American Psychological Association. (2017). *Guidelines for education and training at the doctoral and postdoctoral level in consulting psychology (CP)/organizational consulting psychology (OCP).* https://www.apa.org/about/policy/education-training.pdf

American Psychological Association. (2021). *Inclusive language guidelines.* https://www.apa.org/about/apa/equity-diversity-inclusion/language-guidelines.pdf

American Psychological Association. (2022a). *Face the numbers: Moving beyond financial debt.* https://www.apa.org/topics/stress/money?msclkid=6c65cf83b1c611ec8cd09ca45862283b

American Psychological Association, APA Task Force on Guidelines for Assessment and Intervention With Persons With Disabilities. (2022b). *Guidelines for assessment and intervention with persons with disabilities.* https://www.apa.org/about/policy/guidelines-assessment-intervention-disabilities.pdf

Amir, M. (1971). *Patterns in forcible rape.* University of Chicago Press.

Ancis, J. R., & Marshall, D. S. (2010). Using a multicultural framework to assess supervisees' perceptions of culturally competent supervision. *Journal of Counseling and Development, 88*(3), 277–284. https://doi.org/10.1002/j.1556-6678.2010.tb00023.x

Andrews, E. E. (2020). *Disability as diversity: Developing cultural competence.* Oxford University Press.

Andrews, E. E., Forber-Pratt, A. J., Mona, L. R., Lund, E. M., Pilarski, C. R., & Balter, R. (2019). #SaytheWord: A disability culture commentary on the erasure of "disability." *Rehabilitation Psychology, 64*(2), 111–118. https://doi.org/10.1037/rep0000258

Andrews, E. E., Powell, R. M., & Ayers, K. (2022). The evolution of disability language: Choosing terms to describe disability. *Disability and Health Journal, 15*(3), Article 101328. Advance online publication. https://doi.org/10.1016/j.dhjo.2022.101328

Asaoka, D. (2020). A behavioral analysis of whistleblowing at Japanese firms. *Humanities & Social Sciences Communications, 7*(1), Article 95. https://doi.org/10.1057/s41599-020-00588-7

Asch, S. E. (1956). Studies of independence and conformity: A minority of one against a unanimous majority. *Psychological Monographs, 70*(9), 1–70. https://doi.org/10.1037/h0093718

Barnett, L. (Ed.). (2009). *When death enters the therapeutic space: Existential perspectives in psychotherapy and counselling.* Routledge.

Bartkowski, J. P. (1998). Claims-making and typifications of voodoo as a deviant religion: Hex, lies, and videotape. *Journal for the Scientific Study of Religion, 37*(4), 559–579. https://doi.org/10.2307/1388141

Bass, A. (1989, April 3). Sexual abuse of patients—Why?: High incidence may be due to therapists' sense of impunity, inaction by professional groups. *The Boston Globe,* pp. 27–28.

Bayoumi, M. (2015). *This Muslim American life: Dispatches from the war on terror.* New York University Press.

Becker, E. (2007). *The denial of death.* Free Press. (Original work published 1973)

Bender, M. C. (2021). *"Frankly, we did win this election": The inside story of how Trump lost.* Twelve.

Berger, L. M., Collins, J. M., & Cuesta, L. (2016). Household debt and adult depressive symptoms in the United States. *Journal of Family and Economic Issues, 37*(1), 42–57. https://doi.org/10.1007/s10834-015-9443-6

Berlinger, J. (Director). (2006, November 30). Dave Chappelle + Maya Angelou (Season 2, Episode 6) [TV series episode]. In A. Fried & C. Walters (Producers), *Iconoclasts.* RadicalMedia. https://pro.imdb.com/title/tt0874578/?rfcons_tt_atf&ref_=cons_tt_atf

Bernard, J. M., & Goodyear, R. K. (2019). *Fundamentals of clinical supervision* (6th ed.). Pearson.

Borders, L. D., & Brown, L. L. (2022). *The new handbook of counseling supervision.* Routledge. https://doi.org/10.4324/9781003251583

Bouhoutsos, J., Holroyd, J., Lerman, H., Forer, B. R., & Greenberg, M. (1983). Sexual intimacy between psychotherapists and patients. *Professional Psychology: Research and Practice, 14*(2), 185–196. https://doi.org/10.1037/0735-7028.14.2.185

Bowler, G. Q., & Bowler, G. (2017). *Christmas in the crosshairs: Two thousand years of denouncing and defending the world's most celebrated holiday.* Oxford University Press.

Brewster, M. E., Hammer, J., Sawyer, J. S., Eklund, A., & Palamar, J. (2016). Perceived experiences of atheist discrimination: Instrument development and evaluation. *Journal of Counseling Psychology, 63*(5), 557–570. https://doi.org/10.1037/cou0000156

Brewster, M. E., Velez, B. L., Geiger, E. F., & Sawyer, J. S. (2020). It's like herding cats: Atheist minority stress, group involvement, and psychological outcomes. *Journal of Counseling Psychology, 67*(1), 1–13. https://doi.org/10.1037/cou0000392

Brown, L. S. (2016). *Supervision essentials for the feminist psychotherapy model of supervision.* American Psychological Association. https://doi.org/10.1037/14878-000

Brown, L. S., & Courtois, C. A. (2021). Sexual misconduct in the feminist therapy realm. In A. Steinberg, J. L. Alpert, & C. A. Courtois (Eds.), *Sexual boundary violations in psychotherapy: Facing therapist indiscretions, transgressions, and misconduct* (pp. 141–153). American Psychological Association. https://doi.org/10.1037/0000247-009

Brown, O., Elkonin, D., & Naicker, S. (2013). The use of religion and spirituality in psychotherapy: Enablers and barriers. *Journal of Religion and Health, 52*(4), 1131–1146. https://doi.org/10.1007/s10943-011-9551-z

Brownfain, J. J. (1971). The APA professional liability insurance program. *American Psychologist, 26*(7), 648–652. https://doi.org/10.1037/h0032052

Bryant-Davis, T., & Comas-Díaz, L. (Eds.). (2016). *Womanist and mujerista psychologies: Voices of fire, acts of courage.* American Psychological Association. https://doi.org/10.1037/14937-000

Buote, L. C., Wada, K., Russell-Mayhew, S., & Feldstain, A. (2022). Maid in Canada: Controversies, guidelines, and the role of psychologists in relation to Bill C-14. *Canadian Psychology, 63*(1), 126–137. https://doi.org/10.1037/cap0000286

Callahan, J. L., & Love, P. K. (2020). Introduction to the special issue: Supervisee perspectives of supervision processes [Editorial]. *Journal of Psychotherapy Integration, 30*(1), 1–8. https://doi.org/10.1037/int0000199

Capawana, M. R., & Walla, P. (Reviewing Ed.). (2016). Intimate attractions and sexual misconduct in the therapeutic relationship: Implications for socially just practice. *Cogent Psychology, 3*(1), Article 1194176. https://doi.org/10.1080/23311908.2016.1194176

Chavez-Dueñas, N. Y., & Adames, H. Y. (2021). Intersectionality Awakening Model of Womanista: A transnational treatment approach for Latinx women. *Women & Therapy, 44*(1–2), 83–100. https://doi.org/10.1080/02703149.2020.1775022

Chavez-Dueñas, N. Y., & Adames, H. Y. (in press). Death, beginning eternity: Aztecs and the afterlife. In J. W. Ellor & H. Harris (Eds.), *Routledge encyclopedia of death, dying and bereavement*. Routledge Press.

Chavez-Dueñas, N. Y., Adames, H. Y., Perez-Chavez, J. G., & Salas, S. P. (2019). Healing ethno-racial trauma in Latinx immigrant communities: Cultivating hope, resistance, and action. *American Psychologist, 74*(1), 49–62. https://doi.org/10.1037/amp0000289

Chrisman, S. A. (Ed.). (2015). *True ladies and proper gentlemen: Victorian etiquette for modern-day mothers and fathers, husbands and wives, boys and girls, teachers and students, and more.* Skyhorse Publishing.

Clark, E., & Bennett, K. (2021). Sexual boundary violations outside of cisgender–heterosexual dyads. In A. Steinberg, J. L. Alpert, & C. A. Courtois (Eds.), *Sexual boundary violations in psychotherapy: Facing therapist indiscretions, transgressions, and misconduct* (pp. 219–236). American Psychological Association. https://doi.org/10.1037/0000247-013

Collins, P. H. (2000). *Black feminist thought: Knowledge, consciousness, and the politics of empowerment* (2nd ed.). Routledge.

Comas-Díaz, L. (2007). Ethnopolitical psychology: Healing and transformation. In E. Aldarondo (Ed.), *Advancing social justice through clinical practice* (pp. 91–118). Lawrence Erlbaum Publishers.

Comas-Díaz, L. (2021). Afro-Latinxs: Decolonization, healing, and liberation. *Journal of Latina/o Psychology, 9*(1), 65–75. https://doi.org/10.1037/lat0000164

Combahee River Collective. (1995). Combahee River Collective statement. In B. Guy-Sheftall (Ed.), *Words of fire: An anthology of African American feminist thought* (pp. 232–240). New Press.

Cooper, B. (2018). *Eloquent rage: A Black feminist discovers her superpower.* St. Martin's Press.

Corr, C. A. (2019). Should we incorporate the work of Elisabeth Kübler-Ross in our current teaching and practice and, if so, how? *Journal of Death and Dying, 83*(4), 706–728. https://doi.org/10.1177/0030222819865397

Crenshaw, K. W. (1991). Mapping the margins: Intersectionality, identity politics, and violence against Women of Color. *Stanford Law Review, 43*(6), 1241–1299. https://doi.org/10.2307/1229039

Cross, R. J. (1991). Helping adolescents learn about sexuality. *SIECUS Report, 19*, 6–11.

Dahlberg, C. C. (1970). Sexual contact between patient and therapist. *Contemporary Psychoanalysis, 6*(2), 107–124. https://doi.org/10.1080/00107530.1970.10745180

David, E. J. R., & Derthick, A. O. (2018). *The psychology of oppression.* Springer Publishing Company.

Davidson, V. (1977). Psychiatry's problem with no name: Therapist-patient sex. *American Journal of Psychoanalysis, 37*(1), 43–50. https://doi.org/10.1007/BF01252822

Delaney, H. D., Miller, W. R., & Bisonó, A. M. (2007). Religiosity and spirituality among psychologists: A survey of clinician members of the American Psychological Association. *Professional Psychology: Research and Practice, 38*(5), 538–546. https://doi.org/10.1037/0735-7028.38.5.538

Demby, G., & Bates, K. G. (Hosts). (2019, May 15). Anger: The Black woman's "superpower" [Audio podcast episode]. In *Code Switch.* NPR. https://www.npr.org/transcripts/723322372

De Montaigne, M. (1994). *The essays: A selection.* Penguin. (Original work published 1580)

Detert, J. R., & Treviño, L. K. (2010). Speaking up to higher-ups: How supervisors and skip-level leaders influence employee voice. *Organization Science, 21*(1), 249–270. https://doi.org/10.1287/orsc.1080.0405

Dew, J., Britt, S., & Huston, S. (2012). Examining the relationship between financial issues and divorce. *Family Relations, 61*(4), 615–628. https://doi.org/10.1111/j.1741-3729.2012.00715.x

Drinane, J. M., Wilcox, M. M., Cabrera, L., & Black, S. W. (2021). To conceal or not to conceal: Supervisee and client identity processes in clinical supervision. *Psychotherapy, 58*(4), 429–436. https://doi.org/10.1037/pst0000387

Dunn, D. S., & Andrews, E. E. (2015). Person-first and identity-first language: Developing psychologists' cultural competence using disability language. *American Psychologist, 70*(3), 255–264. https://doi.org/10.1037/a0038636

Eckerd, L. M. (2009). Death and dying course offerings in psychology: A survey of nine Midwestern states. *Death Studies, 33*(8), 762–770. https://doi.org/10.1080/07481180902961211

Edgell, P., Gerteis, J., & Hartmann, D. (2006). Atheists as "other": Moral boundaries and cultural membership in American society. *American Sociological Review, 71*(2), 211–234. https://doi.org/10.1177/000312240607100203

Ekins, E. E. (2020, July 22). *Poll: 62% of Americans say they have political views they're afraid to share.* Cato Institute. https://www.cato.org/survey-reports/poll-62-americans-say-they-have-political-views-theyre-afraid-share

Estrich, S. (1987). *Real rape.* Harvard University Press.

Falender, C. A., & Shafranske, E. P. (2020). Consultation in psychology: A distinct professional practice. In C. A. Falender & E. P. Shafranske (Eds.), *Consultation in psychology: A competency-based approach* (pp. 11–35). American Psychological Association. https://doi.org/10.1037/0000153-002

Falender, C. A., & Shafranske, E. P. (2021). *Clinical supervision: A competency-based approach* (2nd ed.). American Psychological Association. https://doi.org/10.1037/0000243-000

Fang, M. L., Sixsmith, J., Sinclair, S., & Horst, G. (2016). A knowledge synthesis of culturally- and spiritually-sensitive end-of-life care: Findings from a scoping review. *BMC Geriatrics, 16*(1), Article 107. https://doi.org/10.1186/s12877-016-0282-6

Faulkner, W. (2011). *Requiem for a nun.* Vintage. (Original work published 1950)

Feldman-Summers, S., & Jones, G. (1984). Psychological impacts of sexual contact between therapists or other health care practitioners and their clients. *Journal of Consulting and Clinical Psychology, 52*(6), 1054–1061. https://doi.org/10.1037/0022-006X.52.6.1054

Fennell, R., & Grant, B. (2019). Discussing sexuality in health care: A systematic review. *Journal of Clinical Nursing, 28*(17–18), 3065–3076. https://doi.org/10.1111/jocn.14900

Forer, B. (1980, February). *The psychotherapeutic relationship: 1968* [Paper presentation]. Annual meeting of the California State Psychological Association, Pasadena, CA, United States.

Frankenberg, R. (1997). *Displacing Whiteness: Essays in social and cultural criticisms.* Duke University Press.

Frazier, R. E., & Hansen, N. D. (2009). Religious/spiritual psychotherapy behaviors: Do we do what we believe to be important? *Professional Psychology: Research and Practice, 40*(1), 81–87. https://doi.org/10.1037/a0011671

Freud, S. (1965). *New introductory lectures on psychoanalysis.* J. Strachey (Ed. & Trans.). W. W. Norton & Company. (Original work published 1917)

Friedman, J., & Tager, J. (2021). *Educational gag orders: Legislative restrictions on the freedom to read, learn, and teach.* PEN America. https://pen.org/report/educational-gag-orders/?mc_cid=afacf1d165

Frye, M. (2019). Oppression. In T. Ball, R. Dagger, & D. I. O'Neill (Eds.), *Ideals and ideologies* (11th ed., pp. 411–419). Routledge. https://doi.org/10.4324/9780429286827-67

Gamino, L. A., & Ritter, R. H., Jr. (2009). *Ethical practice in grief counseling.* Springer Publishing Company.

Gansen, H. M. (2017). Reproducing (and disrupting) heteronormativity: Gendered sexual socialization in preschool classrooms. *Sociology of Education, 90*(3), 255–272. https://doi.org/10.1177/0038040717720981

Gechtman, L. (1989). Sexual contact between social workers and their clients. In G. O. Gabbard (Ed.), *Sexual exploitation in professional relationships* (pp. 27–38). American Psychiatric Press.

Gerteis, J., Hartmann, D., & Edgell, P. (2020). Racial, religious, and civic dimensions of anti-Muslim sentiment in America. *Social Problems, 67*(4), 719–740. https://doi.org/10.1093/socpro/spz039

Gervais, W. M., Shariff, A. F., & Norenzayan, A. (2011). Do you believe in atheists? Distrust is central to anti-atheist prejudice. *Journal of Personality and Social Psychology, 101*(6), 1189–1206. https://doi.org/10.1037/a0025882

Gibson, A. S., Ellis, M. V., & Friedlander, M. L. (2019). Toward a nuanced understanding of nondisclosure in psychotherapy supervision. *Journal of Counseling Psychology, 66*(1), 114–121. https://doi.org/10.1037/cou0000295

Gibson, J. (2006). *The war on Christmas: How the liberal plot to ban the sacred Christian holiday is worse than you thought.* Sentinel.

Gibson, J. L., & Sutherland, J. L. (2020). Keeping your mouth shut: Spiraling self-censorship in the United States. *SSRN.* https://doi.org/10.2139/ssrn.3647099

Gómez, J. M., Noll, L. K., Adams-Clark, A. A., & Courtois, C. A. (2021). When colleagues betray: The harm of sexual boundary violations in psychotherapy extends beyond the victim. In A. Steinberg, J. L. Alpert, & C. A. Courtois (Eds.), *Sexual boundary violations in psychotherapy: Facing therapist indiscretions, transgressions, and misconduct* (pp. 297–315). American Psychological Association.

Graham, D. A. (2021, July 10). The rise of anti-history. *The Atlantic.* https://www.theatlantic.com/ideas/archive/2021/07/republicans-anti-history-marjorie-taylor-greene/619403/

Grote, C. L., & Heffelfinger, A. K. (2022). Preventing and managing difficult issues in supervision. In K. J. Stucky, D. Bodin, & S. S. Bush (Eds.), *Supervision in neuropsychology: Practical, ethical, and theoretical considerations* (pp. 83–102). Oxford University Press. https://doi.org/10.1093/oso/9780190088163.003.0005

Grzanka, P. R., Gonzalez, K. A., & Spanierman, L. B. (2019). White supremacy and counseling psychology: A critical–conceptual framework. *The Counseling Psychologist, 47*(4), 478–529. https://doi.org/10.1177/0011000019880843

Hare, C., & Poole, K. T. (2014). The polarization of contemporary American politics. *Polity, 46*(3), 411–429. https://doi.org/10.1057/pol.2014.10

Harris, E. A., & Alter, A. (2022, January 30). Book ban efforts are spreading across the US. *The New York Times.* https://www.nytimes.com/2022/01/30/books/book-ban-us-schools.html

Harris, K. A., Howell, D. S., & Spurgeon, D. W. (2018). Faith concepts in psychology: Three 30-year definitional content analyses. *Psychology of Religion and Spirituality, 10*(1), 1–29. https://doi.org/10.1037/rel0000134

Harris, S. M., & Hays, K. W. (2008). Family therapist comfort with and willingness to discuss client sexuality. *Journal of Marital and Family Therapy, 34*(2), 239–250. https://doi.org/10.1111/j.1752-0606.2008.00066.x

Harrison, E. (2022, January 28). Tennessee school board's "demented" move to ban Holocaust novel *Maus* met with bafflement and anger. *Yahoo! News.* https://ca.news.yahoo.com/tennessee-school-board-demented-move-075505023.html

Hathaway, W. L., Scott, S. Y., & Garver, S. A. (2004). Assessing religious/spiritual functioning: A neglected domain in clinical practice? *Professional Psychology: Research and Practice, 35*(1), 97–104. https://doi.org/10.1037/0735-7028.35.1.97

Hazelbaker, T., & Mistry, R. S. (2022). Negotiating Whiteness: Exploring White elementary school-age children's racial identity development. *Social Development.* Advance online publication. https://doi.org/10.1111/sode.12602

Helms, J. E. (1990). *Black and White racial identity: Theory, research, and practice.* Greenwood Press.

Helms, J. E. (2008). *A race is a nice thing to have: A guide to being a White person or understanding the White persons in your life* (2nd ed.). Microtraining Associates.

Helms, J. E. (2016). An election to save White heterosexual male privilege. *Latinx Psychology Today, 3*(2), 6–7.

Helms, J. E. (2017). The challenge of making Whiteness visible: Reactions to four Whiteness articles. *The Counseling Psychologist, 45*(5), 717–726. https://doi.org/10.1177/0011000017718943

Helms, J. E. (2019). *A race is a nice thing to have: A guide to being a White person or understanding the White persons in your life* (3rd ed.). Cognella.

Henderson, D. J. (1975). Incest. In A. M. Freedman, H. I. Kaplan, & B. J. Sadock (Eds.), *Comprehensive textbook of psychiatry* (pp. 1530–1539). Williams & Wilkins.

Herman, J. L. (1981). *Father–daughter incest.* Harvard University Press.

Hixenbaugh, M., & Hylton, A. (2021, October 14). Southlake school leader tells teachers to balance Holocaust books with "opposing" views: Teachers in the Carroll school district say they fear being punished for stocking classrooms with books dealing with racism, slavery and now the Holocaust. *NBC News.* https://www.nbcnews.com/news/us-news/southlake-texas-holocaust-books-schools-rcna2965?cid=sm_npd_nn_fb_ma

Hodge, B. (2013). *The War on Christmas: Battles in faith, tradition, and religious expression.* New Leaf Publishing Group.

Homan, P., Brown, T. H., & King, B. (2021). Structural intersectionality as a new direction for health disparities research. *Journal of Health and Social Behavior, 62*(3), 350–370. https://doi.org/10.1177/00221465211032947

Huxley, T. H. (2011). *Darwiniana: Collected essays.* Cambridge University Press. (Original work published 1893)

Inman, A. G., & Ladany, N. (2014). Multicultural competencies in psychotherapy supervision. In F. T. L. Leong, L. Comas-Díaz, G. C. Nagayama Hall, V. C. McLoyd, & J. E. Trimble (Eds.), *APA handbook of multicultural psychology: Vol. 2. Applications and training* (pp. 643–658). American Psychological Association. https://doi.org/10.1037/14187-036

Jackall, R. (1988). *Moral mazes: The world of corporate managers.* Oxford University Press.

Jackson, E. R., Shanafelt, T. D., Hasan, O., Satele, D. V., & Dyrbye, L. N. (2016). Burnout and alcohol abuse/dependence among US medical students. *Academic Medicine, 91*(9), 1251–1256. https://doi.org/10.1097/ACM.0000000000001138

Jernigan, M. M., Green, C. E., Helms, J. E., Perez-Gualdron, L., & Henze, K. (2010). An examination of People of Color supervision dyads: Racial identity matters as much as race. *Training and Education in Professional Psychology, 4*(1), 62–73. https://doi.org/10.1037/a0018110

Johnson, D. K. (2013, December 22). Sorry Fox News, there is no War on Christmas and Santa isn't White. *LSE American Politics and Policy.* https://blogs.lse.ac.uk/usappblog/2013/12/22/fox-news-christmas/

Johnson, J. (2015, December 7). Trump calls for "total and complete shutdown of Muslims entering the United States." *The Washington Post*. https://www.washingtonpost.com/news/post-politics/wp/2015/12/07/donald-trump-calls-for-total-and-complete-shutdown-of-muslims-entering-the-united-states/

Johnson, S. M., Cramer, R. J., Conroy, M. A., & Gardner, B. O. (2014). The role of and challenges for psychologists in physician assisted suicide. *Death Studies*, *38*(9), 582–588. https://doi.org/10.1080/07481187.2013.820228

Jones, A. M. (2021). Letters to their attackers: Using counterstorytelling to share how Black women respond to racial microaggressions at a historically White institution. *International Journal of Qualitative Studies in Education*. https://doi.org/10.1080/09518398.2021.1942292

Jones, C. P. (2000). Levels of racism: A theoretic framework and a gardener's tale. *American Journal of Public Health*, *90*(8), 1212–1215. https://doi.org/10.2105/AJPH.90.8.1212

Jones, E. E. (1961). *The life and work of Sigmund Freud* (L. Trilling & S. Marcus, Trans. & Eds.). Basic Books.

Jones, J. M. (1972). *Prejudice and racism*. Addison-Wesley Publishing Co.

Jones, J. M. (1997). *Prejudice and racism* (2nd ed.). McGraw-Hill Companies.

Jones, S. C., & Neblett, E. W., Jr. (2019). The impact of racism on the mental health of People of Color. In M. T. Williams, D. C. Rosen, & J. W. Kanter (Eds.), *Eliminating race-based mental health disparities: Promoting equity and culturally responsive care across settings* (pp. 79–97). Context Press/New Harbinger Publications.

Joshi, K. Y. (2020). *White Christian privilege: The illusion of religious equality in America*. New York University Press.

Kardiner, S. H., Fuller, M., & Mensch, I. N. (1973). A survey of physicians' attitudes and practices regarding erotic and nonerotic contact with patients. *American Journal of Psychiatry*, *130*(10), 1324–1325. https://doi.org/10.1176/ajp.130.10.1077

Karson, M. (2018). *What every therapist needs to know*. Rowman & Littlefield.

Kennedy, F. (1970). Institutionalized oppression vs. the female. In R. Morgan (Ed.), *Sisterhood is powerful: An anthology of writings from the women's liberation movement* (pp. 438–446). Random House.

King, M. L., Jr. (n.d.). *Martin Luther King Jr. quotes*. https://www.azquotes.com/quote/158975

Knox, S., Burkard, A. W., Johnson, A. J., Suzuki, L. A., & Ponterotto, J. G. (2003). African American and European American therapists' experiences of addressing race in cross-racial psychotherapy dyads. *Journal of Counseling Psychology*, *50*(4), 466–481. https://doi.org/10.1037/0022-0167.50.4.466

Komischke-Konnerup, K. B., Zachariae, R., Johannsen, M., Nielsen, L. D., & O'Connor, M. (2021). Co-occurrence of prolonged grief symptoms and symptoms of depression, anxiety, and posttraumatic stress in bereaved adults:

A systematic review and meta-analysis. *Journal of Affective Disorders Reports, 4,* Article 100140. https://doi.org/10.1016/j.jadr.2021.100140

Kromrey, B. (2021). *Encountering death: A training proposal for psychologists addressing death anxiety and end-of-life care* [Unpublished doctoral dissertation]. University of Denver. https://digitalcommons.du.edu/capstone_masters/415/

Ladany, N., Friedlander, M. L., & Nelson, M. L. (2016). *Supervision essentials for the critical events in psychotherapy supervision model.* American Psychological Association. https://doi.org/10.1037/14916-000

Lantz, J. (1999). Meaning and the post-parental couple. *Journal of Religion and Health, 38*(1), 53–66. https://doi.org/10.1023/A:1022916016375

Lewis, J. A., Williams, M. G., Peppers, E. J., & Gadson, C. A. (2017). Applying intersectionality to explore the relations between gendered racism and health among Black women. *Journal of Counseling Psychology, 64*(5), 475–486. https://doi.org/10.1037/cou0000231

Lorde, A. (1997). The uses of anger. *Women's Studies Quarterly, 25*(1/2), 278–285. https://www.jstor.org/stable/40005441

Love, E. (2017). *Islamophobia and racism in America.* New York University Press.

Lung, S. L. M., Wincentak, J., Gan, C., Kingsnorth, S., Provvidenza, C., & McPherson, A. C. (2021). Are healthcare providers and young people talking about sexuality? A scoping review to characterize conversations and identify barriers. *Child: Care, Health and Development, 47*(6), 744–757. https://doi.org/10.1111/cch.12892

Magyar-Russell, G. (2020). Delivering psychological services to religious and spiritual clients. In J. Zimmerman, J. E. Barnett, & L. F. Campbell (Eds.), *Bringing psychotherapy to the underserved: Challenges and strategies* (pp. 145–162). Oxford University Press. https://doi.org/10.1093/med-psych/9780190912727.003.0007

Marina, S., Wainwright, T., & Ricou, M. (2021). Views of psychologists about their role in hastened death. *OMEGA—Journal of Death and Dying.* https://doi.org/10.1177/00302228211045166

Martherus, J. L., Martinez, A. G., Piff, P. K., & Theodoridis, A. G. (2021). Party animals? Extreme partisan polarization and dehumanization. *Political Behavior, 43*(2), 517–540. https://doi.org/10.1007/s11109-019-09559-4

Mbiti, S. J. (1991). *Introduction to African religion* (2nd ed.). Waveland Press.

McCann, C. J., & Adames, H. Y. (2013). Dying other, dying self: Creating culture and meaning in palliative healthcare. *Palliative and Supportive Care, 11*(4), 289–293. https://doi.org/10.1017/S1478951512000557

McCarthy, J. (2015, June 22). *In U.S., socialist presidential candidates least appealing.* https://www.gallup.com/poll/183713/socialist-presidential-candidates-leastappealing.aspx

McWhorter, J. (2020, September 1). Academics are really, really worried about their freedom. *The Atlantic.* https://www.theatlantic.com/ideas/archive/2020/09/academics-are-really-really-worried-about-their-freedom/615724/

Mendoza, S. (2021). Paying for love in the helping professions: Contradictions inherent in charging fees for psychotherapy. In B. Bishop, A. Dickinson, A. Foster, & J. Klein (Eds.), *Difference: An avoided topic in practice* (pp. 115–128). Routledge.

Milne, D. L., Leck, C., & Choudhri, N. Z. (2009). Collusion in clinical supervision: Literature review and case study in self-reflection. *The Cognitive Behaviour Therapist*, *2*(2), 106–114. https://doi.org/10.1017/S1754470X0900018X

Milne, D. L., & Watkins, C. E., Jr. (2014). Defining and understanding clinical supervision: A functional approach. In C. E. Watkins, Jr., & D. L. Milne (Eds.), *The Wiley international handbook of clinical supervision* (pp. 3–19). John Wiley & Sons. https://doi.org/10.1002/9781118846360.ch1

Miranda, R., & Jeglic, E. L. (Eds.). (2021). *Handbook of youth suicide prevention: Integrating research into practice.* Springer. https://doi.org/10.1007/978-3-030-82465-5

Moise, N., & Hankerson, S. (2021). Addressing structural racism and inequities in depression care. *JAMA Psychiatry*, *78*(10), 1061–1062. https://doi.org/10.1001/jamapsychiatry.2021.1810

Moore-Berg, S. L., Hameiri, B., & Bruneau, E. (2020). The prime psychological suspects of toxic political polarization. *Current Opinion in Behavioral Sciences*, *34*, 199–204. https://doi.org/10.1016/j.cobeha.2020.05.001

Muran, J. C., Safran, J. D., Gorman, B. S., Samstag, L. W., Eubanks-Carter, C., & Winston, A. (2009). The relationship of early alliance ruptures and their resolution to process and outcome in three time-limited psychotherapies for personality disorders. *Psychotherapy: Theory, Research, Practice, Training, 46*(2), 233–248. https://doi.org/10.1037/a0016085

Nakamura, N., & Logie, C. H. (Eds.). (2020). *LGBTQ mental health: International perspectives and experiences.* American Psychological Association. https://doi.org/10.1037/0000159-000

Native American Rights Fund. (1979, Winter). *"We also have a religion": The American Indian Religious Freedom Act and the Religious Freedom Project of the Native American Rights Fund.* https://www.narf.org/nill/documents/nlr/nlr5-1.pdf

Nelson, G., & Prilleltensky, I. (2010). *Community psychology: In pursuit of liberation and well-being* (2nd ed.). Palgrave Macmillan.

Nelson, T. D. (Ed.). (2017). *Ageism: Stereotyping and prejudice against older persons.* The MIT Press.

Neville, H. A., Awad, G. H., Brooks, J. E., Flores, M. P., & Bluemel, J. (2013). Color-blind racial ideology: Theory, training, and measurement implications in psychology. *American Psychologist*, *68*(6), 455–466. https://doi.org/10.1037/a0033282

Newman, B. M., & Newman, P. R. (2017). *Development through life: A psychosocial approach* (13th ed.). Wadsworth Publishing.

Nickell, N. J., Hecker, L. L., Ray, R. E., & Bercik, J. (1995). Marriage and family therapists' sexual attraction to clients: An exploratory study. *The American Journal of Family Therapy*, *23*(4), 315–327. https://doi.org/10.1080/01926189508251362

Nixon, B., & Quinlan, E. (2022). Asking the hard questions: Psychologists' discomfort with inquiring about sexual abuse histories. *Violence Against Women, 28*(5), 1358–1376. https://doi.org/10.1177/10778012211014558

Nobles, W. W. (n.d.). *Critical concepts.* https://www.drwadenobles.com/

Okun, T. (2021, May). *White supremacy culture—Still here.* https://drive.google.com/file/d/1XR_7M_9qa64zZ00_JyFVTAjmjVU-uSz8/view

Olkin, R. (1999). *What psychotherapists should know about disability.* The Guilford Press.

Owen, J., Drinane, J., Tao, K. W., Adelson, J. L., Hook, J. N., Davis, D., & Fookune, N. (2017). Racial/ethnic disparities in client unilateral termination: The role of therapists' cultural comfort. *Psychotherapy Research, 27*(1), 102–111. https://doi.org/10.1080/10503307.2015.1078517

Owen, J., Tao, K. W., Drinane, J. M., Hook, J. Davis, D. E., & Kune, N. F. (2016). Client perceptions of therapist multicultural orientation: Cultural (missed) opportunities and cultural humility. *Professional Psychology: Research and Practice, 47*(1), 30–37. https://doi.org/10.1037/pro000046

Parham, T. A., & Sue, D. W. (2017, February 24). *The fierce urgency of now: A dialogue on where we've been and the road ahead* [Invited plenary, videotaped]. Teachers College, Columbia University, 34th Annual Winter Roundtable on Cultural Psychology and Education, New York, NY, United States. Retrieved May 2022 from https://www.tc.columbia.edu/roundtable2017/#speakers

Peacock, L. (2014, May 13). The real reasons why death is still so hard to talk about with your loved ones. *The Telegraph.* https://www.telegraph.co.uk/women/womens-life/10825710/The-real-reasons-why-death-is-still-so-taboo-hard-to-talk-about-with-your-loved-ones.html

Peiser, J. (2022, January 10). An Indiana GOP state senator said teachers "need to be impartial" during lessons about Nazism and fascism. *The Washington Post.* https://www.washingtonpost.com/nation/2022/01/10/scott-baldwin-indiana-nazism-fascism/

Pew Research Center. (2019a, November 15). *Americans have positive views about religion's role in society, but want it out of politics.* https://www.pewresearch.org/religion/2019/11/15/americans-trust-both-religious-and-nonreligious-people-but-most-rarely-discuss-religion-with-family-or-friends/

Pew Research Center. (2019b, October 17). *In U.S., decline of Christianity continues at rapid pace: An update on America's changing religious landscape.* https://www.pewresearch.org/religion/2019/10/17/in-u-s-decline-of-christianity-continues-at-rapid-pace/

Pope, K. S. (1994). *Sexual involvement with therapists: Patient assessment, subsequent therapy, forensics.* American Psychological Association.

Pope, K. S. (1997). Science as careful questioning: Are claims of a false memory syndrome epidemic based on empirical evidence? *American Psychologist, 52*(9), 997–1006. https://doi.org/10.1037/0003-066X.52.9.997.b

Pope, K. S. (2017). *Five steps to strengthen ethics in organizations and individuals: Effective strategies informed by research and history.* Routledge.

Pope, K. S., Keith-Spiegel, P., & Tabachnick, B. G. (1986). Sexual attraction to clients: The human therapist and the (sometimes) inhuman training system. *American Psychologist, 41*(2), 147–158. https://doi.org/10.1037/0003-066X.41.2.147

Pope, K. S., Keith-Spiegel, P., & Tabachnick, B. G. (2006). Sexual attraction to clients: The human therapist and the (sometimes) inhuman training system. *Training and Education in Professional Psychology, S*(2), 96–111. https://doi.org/10.1037/1931-3918.S.2.96

Pope, K. S., Sonne, J. L., & Greene, B. (2006). *What therapists don't talk about and why: Understanding taboos that hurt us and our clients.* American Psychological Association. https://doi.org/10.1037/11413-000

Pope, K. S., Sonne, J. L., & Holroyd, J. (1993). *Sexual feelings in psychotherapy: Explorations for therapists and therapists-in-training.* American Psychological Association. https://doi.org/10.1037/10124-000

Pope, K. S., & Tabachnick, B. G. (1993). Therapists' anger, hate, fear, and sexual feelings: National survey of therapist responses, client characteristics, critical events, formal complaints, and training. *Professional Psychology: Research and Practice, 24*(2), 142–152. https://doi.org/10.1037/0735-7028.24.2.142

Pope, K. S., Vasquez, M. J. T., Chavez-Dueñas, N. Y., & Adames, H. Y. (2021). *Ethics in psychotherapy and counseling: A practical guide* (6th ed.). John Wiley & Sons.

Porter, N., & Vasquez, M. (1997). Covision: Feminist supervision, process, and collaboration. In J. Worell & N. G. Johnson (Eds.), *Shaping the future of feminist psychology: Education, research, and practice* (pp. 155–171). American Psychological Association. https://doi.org/10.1037/10245-007

Pyke, K. D. (2010). What is internalized racial oppression and why don't we study it? Acknowledging racism's hidden injuries. *Sociological Perspectives, 53*(4), 551–572. https://doi.org/10.1525/sop.2010.53.4.551

Quiñones-Rosado, R. (2007). *Consciousness-in-action: Toward an integral psychology of liberation & transformation.* ilé Publications.

Quiñones-Rosado, R. (2020). Liberation psychology and racism. In L. Comas-Díaz & E. Torres Rivera (Eds.), *Liberation psychology: Theory, method, practice, and social justice* (pp. 53–68). American Psychological Association. https://doi.org/10.1037/0000198-004

Reitsma, L., Boelen, P. A., de Keijser, J., & Lenferink, L. I. M. (2021). Online treatment of persistent complex bereavement disorder, posttraumatic stress disorder, and depression symptoms in people who lost loved ones during the COVID-19 pandemic: Study protocol for a randomized controlled trial and a controlled trial. *European Journal of Psychotraumatology, 12*(1), Article 1987687. https://doi.org/10.1080/20008198.2021.1987687

Reuters. (2019, April 29). *9 recent attacks at U.S. houses of worship* [Slide presentation]. https://www.reuters.com/news/picture/9-recent-attacks-at-us-houses-of-worship-idUSRTX6TNFM

Reyes, G., Barrios, V. R., Banda, R. M., Aronson, B., Claros Berlioz, E. M., & Castañeda, M. E. (2021). "We came together out of necessity": A Latina diaspora group engaging in plática to thrive with dignity in academia. *Journal of Women and Gender in Higher Education, 14*(3), 283–301. https://doi.org/10.1080/26379112.2021.1958221

Richardson, T., Elliott, P., Roberts, R., & Jansen, M. (2017). A longitudinal study of financial difficulties and mental and physical health in a national sample of British undergraduate students. *Community Mental Health Journal, 53*(3), 344–352. https://doi.org/10.1007/s10597-016-0052-0

Robinson, J., Kolves, K., & Sisask, M. (2022). Introduction to the PLOS ONE collection on "Understanding and preventing suicide: Towards novel and inclusive approaches." *PLOS ONE, 17*(3), Article e0264984. https://doi.org/10.1371/journal.pone.0264984

Rozel, J. S., Soliman, L., & Jain, A. (2021). The gun talk: How to have effective conversations with patients and families about firearm injury prevention. In L. S. Zun, K. Nordstrom, & M. P. Wilson (Eds.), *Behavioral emergencies for healthcare providers* (2nd ed., pp. 465–473). Springer.

Sabucedo, P., Evans, C., & Hayes, J. (2020). Perceiving those who are gone: Cultural research on post-bereavement perception or hallucination of the deceased. *Transcultural Psychiatry.* https://doi.org/10.1177/1363461520962887

Samuel, L. R. (2013, June 23). Death, American style: American's uneasy relationship with death and dying goes back almost a century. *Psychology Today.* https://www.psychologytoday.com/us/blog/psychology-yesterday/201306/death-american-style

Santayana, G. (1905). *The life of reason or the phases of human progress: Introduction & reason in commonsense.* Charles Scribner's Sons.

Saracino, R. M., Rosenfeld, B., Breitbart, W., & Chochinov, H. M. (2019). Psychotherapy at the end of life. *The American Journal of Bioethics, 19*(12), 19–28. https://doi.org/10.1080/15265161.2019.1674552

Saroglou, V., Yzerbyt, V., & Kaschten, C. (2011). Meta-stereotypes of groups with opposite religious views: Believers and non-believers. *Journal of Community & Applied Social Psychology, 21*(6), 484–498. https://doi.org/10.1002/casp.1123

Schmitz, W. M., Allen, M. H., Feldman, B. N., Gutin, N. J., Jahn, D. R., Kleespies, P. M., Quinnett, P., & Simpson, S. (2012). Preventing suicide through improved training in suicide risk assessment and care: An American Association of Suicidology task force report addressing serious gaps in U.S. mental health training. *Suicide and Life-Threatening Behavior, 42*(3), 292–304. https://doi.org/10.1111/j.1943-278X.2012.00090.x

Schofield, W. (1971). Psychotherapy: The unknown versus the untold. *Journal of Consulting and Clinical Psychology, 36*(1), 9–11. https://doi.org/10.1037/h0030482

Scholars at Risk. (2021). *Free to think: Report of the Scholars at Risk Academic Freedom Monitoring Project.* https://www.scholarsatrisk.org/wp-content/uploads/2021/12/Scholars-at-Risk-Free-to-Think-2021.pdf

Schultz-Ross, R. A., & Gutheil, T. G. (1997). Difficulties in integrating spirituality into psychotherapy. *Journal of Psychotherapy Practice & Research, 6*(2), 130–138.

Searles, H. F. (1959). Oedipal love in the countertransference. *The International Journal of Psychoanalysis, 40,* 180–190.

Selod, S. (2019). Gendered racialization: Muslim American men and women's encounters with racialized surveillance. *Ethnic and Racial Studies, 42*(4), 552–569. https://doi.org/10.1080/01419870.2018.1445870

Sharma, E., Mazar, N., Alter, A. L., & Ariely, D. (2014). Financial deprivation selectively shifts moral standards and compromises moral decisions. *Organizational Behavior and Human Decision Processes, 123*(2), 90–100. https://doi.org/10.1016/j.obhdp.2013.09.001

Shelton, M. (2020). *Sexual attraction in therapy: Managing feelings of desire in clinical practice.* Routledge.

Shepard, M. (1971). *The love treatment: Sexual intimacy between patients and psychotherapists.* Wyden.

Shively, M. G., & De Cecco, J. P. (1977). Component of sexual identity. *Journal of Homosexuality, 3*(1), 41–48. https://doi.org/10.1300/J082v03n01_04

Simon, J. D., Boyd, R., & Subica, A. M. (2022). Refocusing intersectionality in social work education: Creating a brave space to discuss oppression and privilege. *Journal of Social Work Education, 58*(1), 34–45. https://doi.org/10.1080/10437797.2021.1883492

Simonetti, J. A., Wortzel, H. S., & Matarazzo, B. B. (2021). Therapeutic risk management and firearm-related lethal means safety. *Journal of Psychiatric Practice, 27*(6), 456–465. https://doi.org/10.1097/pra.0000000000000586

Smedley, A., & Smedley, B. D. (2005). Race as biology is fiction, racism as a social problem is real: Anthropological and historical perspectives on the social construction of race. *American Psychologist, 60*(1), 16–26. https://doi.org/10.1037/0003-066X.60.1.16

Smith, E. (2018). Dispatches from the war on Christmas. *Columbia: A Journal of Literature and Art, 56,* 184–195. http://www.jstor.org/stable/45218563

Sommers-Flanagan, J. (2013, March 14). *Through the anger looking glass.* Psychotherapy.net. https://www.psychotherapy.net/blog/title/through-the-anger-looking-glass

Sonne, J. L., & Jochai, D. (2014). The "vicissitudes of love" between therapist and patient: A review of the research on romantic and sexual feelings, thoughts, and behaviors in psychotherapy. *Journal of Clinical Psychology, 70*(2), 182–195. https://doi.org/10.1002/jclp.22069

Sonne, J. L., & Weniger, J. L. (2018). Ethical clinical practice: Negotiating a whole lot of gray in a wise way. In J. N. Butcher & J. M. Hooley (Eds.), *APA handbook of psychopathology: Understanding, assessing, and treating adult mental disorders* (pp. 729–749). American Psychological Association. https://doi.org/10.1037/0000064-030

Spiegelman, A. (1996). *The complete Maus: A survivor's tale.* Pantheon.

Stone, A. A. (1990, March). No good deed goes unpunished. *Psychiatric Times*, pp. 24–27.

Stone, D. F. (2019). "Unmotivated bias" and partisan hostility: Empirical evidence. *Journal of Behavioral and Experimental Economics, 79*, 12–26. https://doi.org/10.1016/j.socec.2018.12.009

Strossen, N. (2020, November). *Resisting cancel culture: Promoting dialogue, debate, and free speech in the college classroom.* American Council of Trustees and Alumni. https://eric.ed.gov/?id=ED610221

Thrower, S. J., Helms, J. E., & Price, M. (2020). Racial dynamics in counselor training: The racial identity social interaction model. *Journal of Counselor Preparation and Supervision, 13*(1). https://doi.org/10.7729/131.1313

Trachtman, R. (2008a). Beyond the fee: Addressing non-fee, money-related issues in psychotherapy and psychoanalysis. *The Candidate, 3*(1), 1–13. https://richardtrachtman.com/pdf/TrachtmanVol3.pdf

Trachtman, R. (2008b). The money taboo in psychotherapy and everyday life. *New Therapist, 58*, 9–17.

Trachtman, R. (2011). *Money and psychotherapy: A guide for mental health professionals.* NASW Press.

Vaccaro, A. (2017). "Trying to act like racism is not there": Women of Color at a predominantly White women's college challenging dominant ideologies by exposing racial microaggressions. *NASPA Journal About Women in Higher Education, 10*(3), 262–280. https://doi.org/10.1080/19407882.2017.1348303

Vasquez, M. J. T., & Johnson, J. D. (2022). *Multicultural therapy: A practice imperative.* American Psychological Association. https://doi.org/10.1037/0000279-000

Vesentini, L., Van Puyenbroeck, H., De Wachter, D., Matthys, F., & Bilsen, J. (2021). Sexual feelings toward clients in the psychotherapeutic relationship: The taboo revealed. *Qualitative Health Research, 31*(5), 999–1011. https://doi.org/10.1177/1049732321990654

Vesentini, L., Van Puyenbroeck, H., De Wachter, D., Matthys, F., & Bilsen, J. (2022). Managing romantic and sexual feelings towards clients in the psychotherapy room in Flanders (Belgium). *Sexual Abuse.* Advance online publication. https://doi.org/10.1177/10790632221098357

Vonnegut, K. (1987). *Bluebeard.* Delacourt Press.

Wasserman, D. (Ed.). (2021). *Oxford textbook of suicidology and suicide prevention* (2nd ed.). Oxford University Press.

Watson-Singleton, N. N. (2017). Strong Black woman schema and psychological distress: The mediating role of perceived emotional support. *Journal of Black Psychology, 43*(8), 778–788. https://doi.org/10.1177/0095798417732414

Wegner, R. (2022, January 27). Tennessee school board's removal of Holocaust book 'Maus' draws international attention. *The Tennessean.* https://www.tennessean.com/story/news/education/2022/01/27/tennessee-school-board-removes-holocaust-mausart-spiegelman/9237260002/

Weinberg, S. K. (1955). *Incest behavior.* Citadel Press.

Wenzel, A. (2021). A cognitive behavioral approach to understanding sexual boundary violations. In A. Steinberg, J. L. Alpert, & C. A. Courtois (Eds.), *Sexual boundary violations in psychotherapy: Facing therapist indiscretions, transgressions, and misconduct* (pp. 105–116). American Psychological Association.

Werth, J. L., Jr. (1999). When is a mental health professional competent to assess a person's decision to hasten death? *Ethics & Behavior, 9*(2), 141–157. https://doi.org/10.1207/s15327019eb0902_5

Werth, J. L., Jr., Benjamin, G. A. H., & Farrenkopf, T. (2000). Requests for physician-assisted death: Guidelines for assessing mental capacity and impaired judgment. *Psychology, Public Policy, and Law, 6*(2), 348–372. https://doi.org/10.1037/1076-8971.6.2.348

West, C. (2008). *Hope on a tightrope: Words & wisdom.* Smiley Books.

Wigmore, J. H. (1970). *Evidence in trials at common law.* Little, Brown. (Original work published 1934)

Wintemute, G. J., Betz, M. E., & Ranney, M. L. (2016). Yes, you can: Physicians, patients, and firearms. *Annals of Internal Medicine, 165*(3), 205–213. https://doi.org/10.7326/M15-2905

Wojtkowiak, J., Lind, J., & Smid, G. E. (2021). Ritual in therapy for prolonged grief: A scoping review of ritual elements in evidence-informed grief interventions. *Frontiers in Psychiatry, 11*, Article 623835. https://doi.org/10.3389/fpsyt.2020.623835

Worden, J. W. (2018). *Grief counseling and grief therapy: A handbook for the mental health practitioner.* Springer.

Worden, J. W., & Proctor, W. (1976). *PDA: Personal death awareness.* Prentice Hall.

Wright, R. H. (1985). The Wright way: Who needs enemies? *Psychotherapy in Private Practice, 3*(2), 111–118. https://doi.org/10.1300/J294v03n02_15

Yager, J., & Kay, J. (2022). Money matters in psychiatric assessment, case formulation, treatment planning, and ongoing psychotherapy: Clinical psycho-economics. *The Journal of Nervous and Mental Disease, 210*(11), 811–817. https://doi.org/10.1097/NMD.0000000000001552

Zmigrod, L., Rentfrow, P. J., & Robbins, T. W. (2020). The partisan mind: Is extreme political partisanship related to cognitive inflexibility? *Journal of Experimental Psychology: General, 149*(3), 407–418. https://doi.org/10.1037/xge0000661

Index

About the Authors

Kenneth S. Pope, PhD, ABPP, is a licensed psychologist. A fellow of the Association for Psychological Science, he served as chair of the ethics committees of the American Board of Professional Psychology (ABPP) and the American Psychological Association (APA). He received the APA Award for Distinguished Contributions to Public Service, the APA Division 12 (Society of Clinical Psychology) Award for Distinguished Professional Contributions to Clinical Psychology, the Canadian Psychological Association's John C. Service Member of the Year Award, and the Ontario Psychological Association's Barbara Wand Award for significant contribution to excellence in professional ethics and standards.

Dr. Pope's authored or coauthored books include *Succeeding as a Therapist: How to Create a Thriving Practice in a Changing World* (with Hector Y. Adames, Nayeli Y. Chavez-Dueñas, and Melba J. T. Vasquez; 2023); the sixth edition of *Ethics in Psychotherapy and Counseling: A Practical Guide* (with Melba J. T. Vasquez, Nayeli Y. Chavez-Dueñas, and Hector Y. Adames; 2021); *Five Steps to Strengthen Ethics in Organizations and Individuals: Effective Strategies Informed by Research and History* (2017); the third edition of *The MMPI, MMPI-2, and MMPI-A in Court: A Practical Guide for Expert Witnesses and Attorneys* (with James N. Butcher and Joyce Seelen; 2006); *What Therapists Don't Talk About and Why: Understanding Taboos That Hurt Us and Our Clients* (with Janet L. Sonne and Beverly Greene; 2006); *How to Survive and Thrive as a Therapist: Information, Ideas, and Resources for Psychologists in Practice* (with Melba J. T. Vasquez; 2005); *Recovered Memories of Abuse: Assessment, Therapy, Forensics* (with Laura S. Brown; 1996); and *Sexual Feelings in Psychotherapy: Explorations for Therapists and Therapists-in-Training* (with Janet L. Sonne and Jean Holroyd; 1993).

Nayeli Y. Chavez-Dueñas, PhD, received her doctorate in clinical psychology from the APA-accredited program at Southern Illinois University at Carbondale. She is a professor at The Chicago School of Professional Psychology, where she serves as the faculty coordinator for the concentration in Latinx mental health in the Counseling Psychology Department. She also is the codirector of the IC-RACE Lab (Immigration Critical Race and Cultural Equity Lab).

Dr. Chavez-Dueñas has coauthored three books: *Succeeding as a Therapist: How to Create a Thriving Practice in a Changing World* (with Hector Y. Adames, Melba J. T. Vasquez, and Kenneth S. Pope; 2023); the sixth edition of *Ethics in Psychotherapy and Counseling: A Practical Guide* (with Kenneth S. Pope, Melba J. T. Vasquez, and Hector Y. Adames; 2021); and *Cultural Foundations and Interventions in Latino/a Mental Health: History, Theory, and Within-Group Differences* (with Hector Y. Adames; 2017). Her research focuses on colorism, skin-color differences, parenting styles, immigration, unaccompanied minors, multiculturalism, and race relations. She has earned a number of awards, including the 2018 APA Distinguished Citizen Psychologist Award. Visit https://icrace.org/ for more information about her lab.

Hector Y. Adames, PsyD, received his doctorate in clinical psychology from the APA-accredited program at Wright State University in Ohio and completed his APA predoctoral internship at the Boston University School of Medicine's Center for Multicultural Training in Psychology. Currently, he is a licensed psychologist and a professor at The Chicago School of Professional Psychology and the codirector of the IC-RACE Lab (Immigration Critical Race and Cultural Equity Lab).

Dr. Adames has coauthored or coedited several books, including *Succeeding as a Therapist: How to Create a Thriving Practice in a Changing World* (with Nayeli Y. Chavez-Dueñas, Melba J. T. Vasquez, and Kenneth S. Pope; 2023); the sixth edition of *Ethics in Psychotherapy and Counseling: A Practical Guide* (with Kenneth S. Pope, Melba J. T. Vasquez, and Nayeli Y. Chavez-Dueñas; 2021); *Caring for Latinxs With Dementia in a Globalized World: Behavioral and Psychosocial Treatments* (with Yvette N. Tazeau; 2020); and *Cultural Foundations and Interventions in Latino/a Mental Health: History, Theory, and Within-Group Differences* (with Nayeli Y. Chavez-Dueñas; 2017). He has earned several awards, including the 2018 Distinguished Emerging Professional Research Award from the Society for the Psychological Study of Culture, Ethnicity and Race (APA Division 45). Visit https://icrace.org/ to learn more about his lab.

Janet L. Sonne, PhD, received her doctorate in clinical psychology from the University of California, Los Angeles (UCLA), and completed her predoctoral internship at the UCLA Neuropsychiatric Institute (now The Jane and Terry

Semel Institute for Neuroscience and Human Behavior). She is a licensed psychologist and an emerita professor in the Department of Psychology at Loma Linda University, where she has taught and supervised clinical psychology graduate students, psychiatry residents, and medical students. A fellow in APA Division 42 (Psychologists in Independent Practice), she has served as a member twice on the APA Ethics Committee and as a member and as chair of the California Psychological Association Ethics Committee. She also has served as an expert consultant/witness in California civil and licensing board (Psychology, Behavioral Sciences, and Nursing) administrative cases regarding standard of care of mental health professionals and potential damages to clients as a result of therapist malpractice.

Dr. Sonne has authored and coauthored several books, book chapters, and journal articles, including the chapter "Ethical Clinical Practice: Negotiating a Whole Lot of Gray in a Wise Way" (with Jennifer L. Weniger) in the *APA Handbook of Psychopathology* (2018); "The 'Vicissitudes of Love' Between Therapist and Patient: A Review of the Research Regarding Romantic and Sexual Feelings, Thoughts, and Behaviors in Psychotherapy" (with Diana Jochai) in the *Journal of Clinical Psychology* (2014); *PsycEssentials: A Pocket Resource for Mental Health Practitioners* (2012); the chapter "Sexualized Relationships" in the *APA Handbook of Ethics in Psychology* (2012); *What Therapists Don't Talk About and Why: Understanding Taboos That Hurt Us and Our Clients* (with Kenneth S. Pope and Beverly Greene; 2006); and *Sexual Feelings in Psychotherapy: Explorations for Therapists and Therapists-in-Training* (with Kenneth S. Pope and Jean Holroyd; 1993).

Beverly A. Greene, PhD, ABPP, is a professor of psychology at St. John's University and founding coeditor of the *Journal of Critical Race and Ethnic Studies*, the journal of St. John's Institute for Critical Race and Ethnic Studies. A practicing clinical psychologist licensed in New York and New Jersey, she is a fellow of APA and nine of its divisions, is board certified in clinical psychology (ABPP), and is a fellow of the American Academy of Clinical Psychology. She has authored more than 100 scholarly publications, of which 12 have received national awards for making significant and distinguished contributions to the psychological literature. She was the founding coeditor of the Society for the Psychology of Sexual Orientation and Gender Diversity (APA Division 44) five-volume book series *Psychological Perspectives on Lesbian, Gay and Bisexual Issues*. Dr. Greene also was coeditor of the award-winning volumes *Psychotherapy With African American Women: Innovations in Psychodynamic Perspectives and Practice* (with Leslie C. Jackson; 2000) and *Women of Color: Integrating Ethnic and Gender Identities in Psychotherapy* (with Lillian Comas-Díaz; 1994). She also coauthored (with Dorith Bordbar; 2010) the article "A Minyan of Women: Family Dynamics, Jewish Identity and Psycho-therapy Practice" in *Women & Therapy*.

Dr. Greene is the recipient of 40 national awards. She also received two APA Presidential Citations for distinguished contributions to scholarship, teaching, mentoring, leadership, service, and advocacy in the form of long-standing pioneering professional contributions to the development of greater under-standings of the intersections of race, gender, and sexual orientation and the development of multiple identity/intersectional paradigms. In 2022, she received the New York City–based Ackerman Institute for the Family's Moving Families Forward Award. Her groundbreaking theoretical formulations have forcefully advocated for the deepening of competencies in working toward the greater integration of psychological theory, research, practice, and social justice and to provide a public health framework for understanding and pro-viding optimal mental health services to many of society's marginalized and disenfranchised members.